Cleveland's Towering Treasure
A Landmark Turns 75

James A. Toman & Daniel J. Cook

To Jeff,
All the best,
James A. Toman

Published by

Cleveland Landmarks Press, Inc.

13610 Shaker Boulevard, Suite 503

Cleveland, Ohio 44120-1592

www.clevelandbook.com

(216) 658 4144

ISBN: 0-936760-20-6

LIBRARY OF CONGRESS NUMBER: 2004095449

Designed by

John Yasenosky

Printed by

Phillips Brothers Printing

Springfield, Illinois

Table of Contents

Cleveland skyline at night, 1978. (Greater Cleveland Growth Association)

Acknowledgments

The authors wish to express their appreciation and indebtedness to the many individuals who invested time and effort to help bring this volume to press.

First and foremost, a most hearty "thank you" goes to Richard E. Karberg. The respected Cleveland historian not only helped with the required research and interviewing, he also shared his considerable collection of Cleveland ephemera, volunteered to do some of the photography, and finally wrote the introduction for this book. Fortified by his love for Cleveland, Karberg's boundless energy and in-depth knowledge of the city were of enormous help in making this work more complete and accurate.

A very special thanks goes to Drew Rolik, archivist for Forest City Enterprises and an expert on the history of the Terminal properties. His commitment to the property turned into yeoman service in helping fill in many gaps in the Terminal story. Don Beck, operations manager for Tower City Center, was also a great help.

Thanks to Bill Barrow and Lynn Bycko of the Special Collections office of the Cleveland State University Library for their guidance in working with the vast collection of Cleveland material archived there. Thanks to Herbert H. Harwood, Jr., historian of the Van Sweringen era, for sharing his knowledge and great collection of photographs with us. We are also grateful to Blaine Hays, foremost historian of Cleveland transportation, for sharing elements of his extensive archive and photo collection.

Many individuals from Forest City Enterprises and Tower City Center were generous in helping us get the details straight. We thank: Albert Ratner, Warren Ornstein, Jane Lisy, Patrick Lott, Emerich Corsi, Dennis Breiding, Paul Moore, James Crosby, James Richardson, Lisa Kreiger, Jack Kuhn, William Voegel, Douglas Bardwell, Alan Krulak, and Rhoda Katzel. Thanks also to Audrey Ratner.

We also thank Professor Emerita Nancy Klein, Richard Latkowski of the General Services Administration, Linda Green of the Chicago Title Insurance Company, Madeline Hayes and John Schillo of the Landmark Office Towers, Arthur Brooks of Baker & Hostetler, Jim Gabler of Renaissance Hotels and Resorts, Sheldon Guren, Judge Lesley Wells of the Federal District Court, David Fischback of The Krill Company, and U. S. Senator George Voinovich.

Thanks to Dr. Mark McKinley for his techno-wizardry. We thank Judith Karberg and Gregory Deegan for help with editing, and we give a special thanks to John Yasenosky who has once again demonstrated his considerable talent in designing a book for Cleveland Landmarks Press, Inc. And lastly, we thank Kathy Cook and Marge Hargus for their continuing support and encouragement.

Dedication We dedicate this book to:

Oris Paxton and Mantis James Van Sweringen, Sheldon Guren, Albert and Audrey Ratner, Ruth Ratner Miller, and Sam Miller, men and women of vision, who have given the Greater Cleveland community much to be proud of.

Founders' Preface

It was in summer 1979 that we founded Cleveland Landmarks Press, Inc. Its origins stemmed from a conversation lamenting the scarcity of books about Cleveland, coupled with regret that the good things about the city were being ignored while its misfortunes were widely heralded.

At the time the city was immersed in a fractious political climate, one which saw Mayor Dennis Kucinich at war with the City Council and the city's business leadership, and which culminated in an August 1978 recall election, further dividing the community. The mayor survived the recall by a scant .2% of the vote, but his woes were not yet over. In November, the City of Cleveland, which had been cash starved for a decade, asked the local banks to roll over its short-term debt. Probably to chasten the mayor, the banks refused to do so, and as a result Cleveland became the first city since the Great Depression to default on its notes. The mood of the community was sour and pessimistic.

Those events formed the background to our conversation. We knew that we could not do much to solve the city's many problems, but we did believe we could at least chronicle some of its happier chapters, perhaps countering, at least in a small way, the negativity that held sway. We would write a book about something in which Clevelanders could and did take pride.

While we concocted a considerable list of topics, it did not require much discussion to determine the subject. The Terminal Tower was Cleveland's proudest symbol, and it was about to celebrate its golden anniversary. The decision made, we started to research and write, and *The Terminal Tower Complex*, our first book, appeared in time for the Terminal's June 1980 golden jubilee celebration.

We had enough faith in our project to raid our meager savings accounts to finance the publishing, and our goal was simply that we would break even. Our modest hopes were more than realized. Clevelanders indeed had an interest in the "good news" about their home town, and the book's sales were brisk.

The success of *The Terminal Tower Complex* led to our being invited to write a golden anniversary book about Cleveland Municipal Stadium in 1981. It too sold well and led to another 20 titles over the course of the last 25 years. In that quarter century others have also taken up the challenge of writing and publishing books about Cleveland. The happy result is that there is no dearth of Cleveland material today.

We could not have sustained our mission if others who shared our love for the city had not joined us in the work of Cleveland Landmarks Press. We are deeply grateful to Kathy Cook, Jack Muslovski, Tom Luckay, Mark Hodermarsky, Blaine Hays, Mike Poplar, Rusty Schneider, Greg and Liz Deegan, Jim Spangler, Bruce Young, Richard and Judith Karberg, Jane Hazen, John Yasenosky, Chris Butler, and Jennifer Rothchild. They have all been part of the Cleveland Landmarks Press family, and the success the company has had is as much theirs as it is ours.

And so, as the silver anniversary of Cleveland Landmarks Press approached and as we thought about what our next project should be, we decided to return to our starting point. The Terminal Tower Complex has reached another milestone, its diamond anniversary, and the last 25 years have seen the reincarnation of the city's most familiar symbol as Tower City Center, with The Avenue as its centerpiece. As the Terminal Tower marks its 75th year, the Center celebrates its 15th.

This volume is a complete revision of *The Terminal Tower Complex*. The intervening years have brought much historical material to light which we happily include here. We also chronicle the significant changes that have taken place since 1980.

It is our hope that for those who missed our first volume, this one will give them an enjoyable look at Cleveland's grand old lady, and for those who read it 25 years ago, this will bring its story up to date.

Cleveland in 2005 is at another point in time when significant challenges are before it. The words with which we closed the preface to our first volume seem just as relevant in today's conditions, and so we repeat the advice of Daniel H. Burnham, the architect who helped develop Cleveland's civic center in the early years of the 20th century: "Make no little plans; they have no magic to stir men's blood and probably themselves will not be realized. Make big plans; aim high in hope and work, remembering that a noble, logical plan once recorded will never die, but long after we are gone will be a living thing asserting itself with growing insistence."

May all Clevelanders once again "make big plans."

 James A. Toman
Daniel J. Cook
Summer 2004

Cleveland's three tallest buildings each guard one of the quadrants of Public Square. (David Kachinko photo)

Introduction

by Richard E. Karberg

By 1910 Cleveland was considered an American industrial metropolis. The rapidly growing city, with a population of 573,872, was a center for iron and steel production, heavy manufacturing, oil refining, the making of clothing, paint and many other products which were important in the industrial expansion America was experiencing at the time.

All of this business activity required a considerable amount of labor. Cleveland business leaders attempted to fill this need by recruiting workers from the rest of the nation, particularly from the South. Still more labor was needed. Cleveland like other rapidly growing American cities turned eastward, recruiting large numbers from Europe. The majority of these new workers arrived at eastern seaboard ports and came to Cleveland by train, disembarking at Cleveland's lakefront Union Depot. The station, dating from 1859, already busy meeting the traveling needs of the businessmen and tourists coming to Cleveland, was taxed to capacity by the additional number of immigrants coming into the city.

In Cleveland, as well as other rapidly growing U.S. cities, the degree of congestion demanded a more radical solution than just adding more tracks and platforms. It resulted in construction of grand railroad stations in Washington, D.C. (1907), Kansas City (1914), New York City (Pennsylvania Station, 1910), Chicago Union Station (1913), and New York's Grand Central Terminal (1913). Because of their size and prominence, these new stations became points of pride and symbols of the growth and wealth of American cities. They were the first buildings seen by travelers approaching their destination.

Originally, Cleveland's new lakefront station was part of the Group Plan of 1903. Architects Burnham and Company from

The impact of the Van Sweringen Union Station plan gave Cleveland a dramatic new skyline. The scene also shows how the development rose on "air rights" over the station's track level. (Herbert H. Harwood photo)

4

"Sorely throb my feet, a-tramping
city pavements (Ah, the springy
sod upon an upland moor!)"

Chicago laid out the preliminary plans, but that station was not to happen. Instead, a Public Square station, championed by Oris P. and Mantis J. Van Sweringen, became the transportation hub for the entire region.

To the Van Sweringen brothers goes the credit for transforming the face of downtown Cleveland as well as eastern suburban areas such as Shaker Heights. In a time of boom and prosperity, their system of rapid transit lines and tightly controlled suburban development was poised to transform Cleveland into a great city.

The Van Sweringen brothers hired a Burnham successor firm, Graham, Anderson, Probst & White to design their station, which was to be the centerpiece of an entire complex covering several city blocks at the southwest quadrant of Public Square.

The interior passageways, arcades, and staircases were elegant, reminiscent of the features of Washington's Union Terminal and New York's Pennsylvania and Grand Central terminals. Grand Central Terminal, because of its size, elegance, and development of the use of air rights, had the most influence on the plans for Cleveland Union Terminal.

New York City's Grand Central trackage fans out below several city blocks. The adjoining streets and the structures along them, including the famed Waldorf Astoria and Biltmore hotels, were built on structural steel bridges over the railroad tracks, using the air rights over the railroad tracks and platforms.

Clevelanders were impressed with the design of this new station which seemed to fit the growth and sophistication emerging in their city in the 1920s. The Van Sweringens apparently instructed Graham, Anderson, Probst & White to plan extravagantly. The complex was to be a city of the future with pedestrian bridges spanning city streets connecting the Terminal group to neighboring buildings. These overhead walkways produced a vision of Cleveland

This rather fanciful image from a booklet advertising a Van Sweringens' suburban development reveals the brothers' interest in both their downtown and Shaker Heights projects. (Richard E. Karberg Collection)

The sleek New York Central *Mercury*, billed as the "train of tomorrow," made its maiden trip between Cleveland and Detroit in 1936. Here it is backing into CUT. (Robert Bachman photo, with permission of TLC Publishing)

very much like that portrayed in Fritz Lang's 1920s German film, *Metropolis*.

The amenities and the ornamentation of Cleveland Union Terminal were in keeping with the luxury found in the Pullman sleeping cars, dining cars, and lounge cars of the era. While planners could not anticipate all the future developments in train design, the amenities of Cleveland Union Terminal certainly met the approval of those who would arrive in the later 1930s on such streamlined trains as New York Central's *Mercury* on the Cleveland-to-Detroit route.

Continuing the theme of amenities for railroad passengers, Van Sweringen associate Charles Bradley was able to entice Fred Harvey, Inc., from Chicago to open a series of shops and fine restaurants in the Terminal Concourse to provide for the needs of travelers as well as for Clevelanders.

Included in the Fred Harvey complex was the legendary English Oak Room. The restaurant was considered the finest in Cleveland, with food and service comparable to dining at the Waldorf Astoria in New York, or on board Cunard and White Star liners crossing the Atlantic, or having dinner at the Dorchester or Savoy hotels in London or the Ritz in Paris.

At the north end of the concourse was the Meeting Place, a sumptuous collection of spaces, including a tea room, fountain, and candy shop, the Jazz Age equivalent of today's food court.

Across the nation, people recognized Cleveland's growing importance in the nation's commerce. By 1930 Cleveland had become the sixth largest city in the U. S., and the new station played a key role in that recognition. The soaring Terminal Tower became a symbol of the wealth, power, and grandeur Cleveland had to offer, and it quickly captured the imagination of many artists of the day.

One such artist was Louis Rosenberg, a graduate of MIT. While an undergraduate

Almost immediately after the Terminal Complex was built, it became the chief icon of the City of Cleveland. This early postcard view shows the tower with its night-time lighting. (Richard E. Karberg Collection)

Photographers were also fascinated by the Terminal. This scene captures the airship *Akron* hovering over the city; the Terminal buildings are at the right. (Richard E. Karberg Collection)

from separate vantage points. In addition to being accurate renderings of the complex, Rosenberg's prints also captured the grandeur and magnificence of this enterprise. The finished plates were sent to Philip Small, and the actual prints were made with the help of Cleveland's Korner and Wood bookstore and gallery.

Unfortunately, the set was never completed due to the financial problems the Vans began to encounter. On November 10, 1930, Rosenberg received word from Small to stop work on the 23rd plate, which would have been a view of the Terminal from the west.

student, Rosenberg had met Philip Small, one of the Vans' favorite architects. It was through Small's influence that the Van Sweringens hired architect and printmaker Rosenberg to create a series of prints recording the construction of Cleveland Union Terminal and the Terminal Tower.

Rosenberg had created prints earlier in his career while on a traveling fellowship. He had studied at the American Academy in Rome and at the Royal College in London and had the academic and artistic qualifications to create superb architectural renderings. His aesthetic taste also corresponded to that of the Vans (for example, Rosenberg's home in Fairfield, Connecticut, closely resembled the styles of homes designed by Van Sweringen-approved architects in Shaker Heights). Between December 1928 and November 1930 Rosenberg produced 22 plates, each documenting the construction of the Terminal Complex at different times and

Another artist of this time who aroused public interest in and appreciation for the Terminal Tower was Margaret Bourke White. Born in New York in 1904, she studied photography at Columbia University with Clarence White, dean of American pictorial photographers. She

The Louis Rosenberg prints of the CUT development, such as this one of the completed Terminal Tower, managed simultaneously to be both accurate and artistic renderings of construction progress. (Shaker Historical Museum)

The New York Central Railroad featured this painting of the Terminal Tower by Leslie Ragan to promote its passenger service to the new Cleveland station, 1930. (Richard E. Karberg Collection)

The camera work of Margaret Bourke-White gave national prominence to the Terminal Tower. This photo is entitled *Public Square Terminal Tower at 5:00, Seen Through a Williamson Building Grille, 1928.* (reproduced with the permission of the estate of Margaret Bourke-White)

A cloudy sky and smog from the industrial valley helped Margaret Bourke-White capture this haunting scene, *Terminal Tower, 1928.* (reproduced with the permission of the estate of Margaret Bourke-White)

went on to Cornell where she received a degree in 1927. It was in Cleveland that she launched her photography career. In the next few years she took the now famous photographs depicting the majesty and daring qualities of the Terminal Tower, which firmly established it as the important symbol of the city.

Her photographs of industrial, commercial, and architectural subjects appeared in leading magazines of the times. Included were her early iconic images of the Terminal which made the structure internationally known. Even details such as the Grille on the 43rd floor became subjects for her camera. Some of these photographs were made into post-

cards and sold at the gift counter on the Observation Porch.

Other artists were also attracted to the Terminal Tower complex as subject matter and created dramatic views in a variety of media.

Throughout the next 50 years the Terminal Tower and its station continued as a symbol of wealth, progress, and prosperity. The addition of the sophisticated Higbee department store in 1931 and the Post Office in 1934 brought additional traffic and attention to the area. The Higbee store was known for its "club like" atmosphere and for its famous Silver Grille. The tea room featured art deco furniture by Louis Rorimer, which

The lights of the Terminal Complex at dusk reflect in the waters of the Cuyahoga River in this postcard view of the landmark. (Richard E. Karberg Collection)

complemented the Small and Rowley design of the room.

The atmosphere created in the Terminal complex was meant to impress and attract home buyers to the Vans' Shaker Heights and country estate development. Homes in Georgian, French, and Tudor styles were beginning to line such streets as Shaker, South Woodland, and Parkland boulevards and the adjacent winding roadways.

Through the anxiety and grimness of World War II and into the faster paced developments in later years, the Terminal remained the most recognizable structure in the city. It continued to be photographed and painted, the subject of many works of art.

But by the 1960s, the city lost its industrial base, and its population fled to suburban areas. And as railroad passenger travel declined, the Terminal lost much of its appeal. Downtown Cleveland remained a center for office space, and Higbee's and other stores continued to attract shoppers, but the Terminal Tower's position as the city's leading structure was being challenged.

Leadership in the city changed, and memories of the Vans and their associates were gone from the scene.

In the 1960s and 1970s it would be another Cleveland family who cared about the city and had a vision to bring about improvements to the urban center of their city. That family was the Ratners, whose vision and hard work carried on the kind of thinking seen in the work of the Van Sweringen brothers.

The Ratowczer family emigrated from Bialystok, Poland, to Cleveland, Ohio, probably arriving at the old Union Depot on the lakefront. After arriving in what would be their new hometown, the family changed its name to Ratner. Of the eight siblings, four combined to start up a lumber business in 1921. Their Forest City stores soon became the Cleveland area's chief source of home improvement products. Forest City founders were brothers Charles, Max, and Leonard, and sister Fannye (Shafran). Over time, the family business grew and branched out into

The Terminal Tower as it is perfectly framed by an upper-story window in the Carl B. Stokes Federal Courthouse. (Richard E. Karberg photo)

construction and real estate development. In venture after venture, the company found success, and in 1960, Forest City Enterprises, Inc. went public. In 2004 Forest City Enterprises had assets of approximately $5.9 billion.

In 1973 Albert B. Ratner, Leonard Ratner's son, became the president of Forest City Enterprises. Albert, concerned with the decline of downtown Cleveland and wanting to help rejuvenate this area of the city, decided there was great opportunity in redeveloping the Terminal Tower Complex. Forest City Enterprises became a partner with U.S. Realty Investments and then eventually sole owner of the complex.

Albert's sister, Ruth Ratner Miller, together with her first husband Samuel H. Miller, who joined Forest City in 1948 and who remains a co-chairman of the firm along with Albert Ratner, also played a key role in the development of what would be called Tower City.

Ruth Ratner Miller received a PhD from CWRU and taught there. She later served as community development director in Ralph Perk's Cleveland mayoral administration. In her work, Ruth developed important contacts which were of great help in making the development of Tower City possible.

Colleagues at Forest City describe Ruth Miller as the project's driving force, involved with its every aspect. It was her idea that Tower City would be the distinctive shopping and entertainment complex in the Midwest. Her friend, Nancy Klein, who taught at CSU and worked with Miller on several projects, stated Ruth wanted Tower City to be a "magnet to bring people downtown."

Securing the Ritz-Carlton Hotel as an anchor for the Tower City Center was another Ratner achievement. Audrey Ratner, Albert's wife, utilizing her background in architecture and design, worked closely with the hotel's interior designer, Frank Nicholson, to insure that the hotel would have a gracious feel. She was involved with the selection of fabrics, decorative items, and furniture. It was important that the hotel exemplify the very best.

Ruth Ratner Miller, in her search for ways to make The Avenue a special place, conducted focus groups comprised mostly of suburban women residing near the rapid lines who would come downtown to shop. When asked to describe their most pleasant shopping experiences, these experienced shoppers did not mention specific stores, but instead spoke of streets such as Fifth Avenue, Regent Street, and Michigan Avenue. The image of an avenue was foremost in their minds. It was from these encounters that the term, The Avenue and the Bobby Short-like lyrics of "Meet Me on the Avenue" emerged. Ruth Miller brought such merchants as Fendi, Gucci, and Barneys to Cleveland to meet the desires of discriminating Clevelanders interested in shopping "On the Avenue" at Tower City Center.

Mary Strassmeyer, columnist for the Cleveland *Plain Dealer*, had always admired the Easter Parades which were held on Euclid Avenue and later in the Fine Arts Garden. Mary revived them on The Avenue, and they became a popular event for downtown Cleveland.

The Ratners also sought ways to link Tower City to the rest of the downtown area. They initiated plans for bridges spanning adjacent streets to link with other downtown structures in the Terminal Tower area. These plans echoed plans proposed by the Van Sweringens in 1930. Regrettably, the Forest City plan for overhead connectors was not approved by the Cleveland Fine Arts Commission, and consequently they were never built.

The cleaning and relighting of the Terminal Tower, which announced the development of Tower City Center, was an event which Senator George Voinovich recalled as one of the most memorable of his political career. The senator, who was mayor of Cleveland at the time, recalls the night of July 13, 1981. Just as the tower's lights came on, a boat filled with analysts who rate municipal bonds, turned the bend on the Cuyahoga River and saw the Terminal Tower suddenly burst into light.

Nestled between the MK-Ferguson Plaza and the Landmark Office Towers are the new buildings of Tower City Center. From left to right are the Ritz-Carlton Hotel/Chase Financial Tower building, the Huron Road entrance to The Avenue, and the Skylight Office Tower. (Richard E. Karberg photo)

The event made an impression on the analysts who began to feel optimistic about the city's future.

For the dual reasons of financing and liability, Tower City properties are divided among several entities. Forest City Enterprises pioneered this way of dividing up the ownership of a particular structure. In order to achieve this separation, ownership surveys and legal documentation had to be created so that separate tax parcels could be created. The distinctive ownership pattern is reminiscent of the complex structure that the Van Sweringens had built earlier.

The Ritz-Carlton Lobby Lounge provides the first indication of the elegance which pervades the entire hotel. (Ritz-Carlton Hotel)

For example, the Greater Cleveland Regional Transit Authority (RTA) was given ownership of the transit station and its tracks, but Forest City Enterprises retained ownership of the central elevator and escalator core leading to its trackage. The dividing of space resulted in multiple owners even on the same level. As an example, the parking lot level includes the following owners, each owning a separate parcel: Tower City Properties, Tower City Parking, and Community Redevelopment Corporation for RTA.

During the 1990s the Federal District Court decided that a new courthouse in Cleveland was essential. The issues of safety and security as well as having sufficient space for the court to conduct an increased volume of business made this decision imperative. Chief Justice Thomas Lambros was determined that the courthouse architecture would be the finest possible.

A number of sites were considered in the downtown area, and the General Services Administration was directed to the Tower City site by Hunter Morrison, then the planning director for the City of Cleveland.

The firm of Kallmann, McKinnell and Wood designed a structure which fulfilled Lambros's vision for a beautiful building that, unlike the old courthouse, would create a distinctive presence on the Cleveland skyline. The Carl B. Stokes Federal Courthouse rises 22 floors, 430 feet, and it contains about 727,000 square feet. The seventh floor roof-line base matches those of adjacent buildings in Tower City.

The completed structure became a distinctive anchor for the property, and it serves as the southwesterly entrance to Tower City Center. The plaza in front of the Courthouse provides the viewer with an idea of what will be the setback from the street for future structures when they are built along Huron Road east of the courthouse. Jim Dine's award-winning sculpture above the entranceway, *Cleveland Venus*, is based on the Venus de Milo statue in the Louvre in Paris.

In many ways the creativity and vision of the Van Sweringens, who earlier in the twentieth century had the vision of transforming the heart of Cleveland into a grand center for Cleveland, was continued in the work of Forest City Enterprises in the late twentieth century.

Bold visions result in lasting achievements.

Ruth Ratner Miller was a key figure in bringing Tower City Center into existence. (Courtesy of Abraham Miller)

The Van Sweringen Brothers

Lakeview Cemetery, situated about 5.5 miles due east of Cleveland's Public Square, is the final resting place of many of the city's legendary leaders. Impressive monuments pay suitable tribute to such giants as Charles Brush, John D. Rockefeller, Jeptha Wade, and President James R. Garfield. The brothers Van Sweringen, Oris Paxton and Mantis James, builders of the Terminal Tower Complex, are buried there too, but the single flat headstone they share gives little evidence of the mighty impact their lives and work have had upon the City of Cleveland. And that is probably the way the reclusive brothers would have wanted it.

The brothers' story begins about 50 miles southwest of Cleveland, in rural Wayne County, Ohio, where James Tower Sweringen and his wife Jennie Curtis Sweringen were struggling to keep their growing family afloat financially. The couple already had three surviving children (a daughter died in infancy), Herbert, Carrie, and Edith, when on April 24, 1879, Oris Paxton Sweringen was born. On July 8, 1881, the family

welcomed its last addition, Mantis James Sweringen.

Looking for better times, James T. Sweringen moved his family north to Geneva, Ohio. It was there in 1886 that Jennie Sweringen died. James then packed up his five children and moved to Cleveland. They settled in a home on Willson Avenue (the street's name was later changed to East 55th Street) near Cedar Avenue.

Brothers Oris Paxton (always called O.P.) and Mantis James (called M.J.) attended first Bolton School and later Fairmount School. Because their father proved unable to hold a full-time job, older brother Herbert provided most of the family's income, and sisters Carrie and Edith assumed the role of mother for the boys. To help with the family finances, O.P. and M.J. got a job delivering the Cleveland *Leader* newspaper to households in the then sparsely populated area that had been

The tombstone marking the grave site of Oris Paxton and Mantis James Van Sweringen, records what was probably to them the most important reality in their lives: They were "brothers." (Richard E. Karberg photo)

The home of the Center Family in the Shakers' North Union Village was a far cry from the structures that would rise there during the Van Sweringen era. (Shaker Historical Museum)

Streetcars climbing Cedar Road Hill opened the Heights area to residential development. (James Spangler collection)

the Shakers' North Union Settlement and which is now Shaker Heights. That early experience was to leave a lasting impression on the brothers.

By 1889 the local Shaker group had shrunk to fewer than 30 members, prompting them to disperse to other Shaker colonies in Ohio and New York. They sold their 1366-acre property to a local real estate firm for $316,000. After the sale,

though, the land saw little development, and customers on the brothers' paper route were few. They trudged through largely open land.

In 1894 the brothers left school and went to work for the Bradley Chemical Company. It was housed in the Society for Savings Building on the northern edge of Public Square. The Society for Savings Building was then the city's tallest "skyscraper," rising 10 stories and 152 feet. Perhaps that early experience in the dominant building in the city's skyline also made an impression on the young brothers.

While both brothers were well endowed with a work ethic, O.P. in particular, the more adventurous of the two, preferred being an entrepreneur rather than an employee. Where O.P. led, M.J. was sure to follow. After a few false starts, O.P. decided that the time was ripe to pursue his ambition for a real estate career.

Following some successful property sales in the city, O.P. concluded that the suburbs held greater profit potential, and so the brothers decided to try their luck in suburban Lakewood, Ohio. Their efforts on Cook Avenue there did not turn out to be the key to their golden dream. Just the opposite, they saw their investment end in foreclosure.

The brothers seemed constitutionally unable to view a setback as a defeat, and so they treated the Lakewood failure as a lesson for their next venture. While they worked to pay back their Lakewood debts, they decided to apply their hard-earned savvy to real estate on the east side of town. To mark their new start, the brothers decided to reattach the "van" prefix that had originally been a part of their family's Dutch ancestry, but which had been earlier dropped to better assimilate into the egalitarian U.S. culture. It was a sound choice, because before long the city's business community and the media were referring to the brothers as "the Vans."

Armed with the aristocratic "Van" prefix and lured by the success which developer

Patrick Calhoun had achieved in developing his upscale garden housing settlement at the top of Cedar Road hill, the brothers turned their real estate attention to Cleveland Heights.

Calhoun's formula there had been to set in place development restrictions that would rule out all but the wealthy, thus

This Fairmount Boulevard home was one of the upscale residences built in the Van Sweringen allotment in Cleveland Heights. (Richard E. Karberg photo)

Oris Paxton (O. P.) Van Sweringen (Shaker Historical Museum)

Mantis James (M. J.) Van Sweringen (Shaker Historical Museum)

The Vans planned Shaker Boulevard as an avenue of stately homes. With the rapid transit line connecting the suburb to downtown Cleveland, the pace of development picked up. (Blaine Hays Collection)

This streetcar, leased from the Cleveland Railway Company, was in service when the rapid transit began operations in 1913. (Blaine Hays Collection)

creating a neighborhood of elegant and distinctive homes. His development along Euclid Heights Boulevard became a magnet for many of the city's most prosperous citizens. Besides the appeal of exclusivity, another element played a key role in his success. In 1896, the Cleveland Electric Railway Company had built a new streetcar line from Euclid Avenue and East 107th Street up Cedar Hill and from there via a median strip along Euclid Heights Boulevard east to Coventry Road. The streetcar line eased the steep climb up Cedar Hill and connected the scenic overlook neighborhood with downtown.

O.P. and M.J. put together a circle of investors, and following Calhoun's tested approach, they set their hand to the development of North Park Boulevard which was located towards the northern end of the Shaker lands (and in what is now Cleveland Heights). Fortune smiled on their venture there and launched the brothers on the road to riches.

The brothers then turned their attention to Fairmount Boulevard. Guided by Patrick Calhoun's example, O.P. and M.J. approached John J. Stanley, president of the Cleveland Railway Company, and asked him to consider building another streetcar line to serve the Fairmount neighborhood. Persuasive salesmen they were, and Stanley agreed to build a new Shaker Lakes streetcar line, later renamed the Fairmount line, from the top of Cedar Hill to Fairmount Boulevard and then along a center reservation to Lee Road (it was extended to Canterbury Road in 1929). The new service opened in 1907. With public transit providing access to the area, the Fairmount Boulevard stretch of stately homes soon became a triumph for the Vans. They were no longer poor men.

Fairmount Boulevard was also at the northern end of the old Shaker Colony, but the brothers' fond memories of their boyhood days on the Shaker plateau drew their attention farther south to the part of the acreage that was still largely empty. The land had changed hands since the original purchase and was then controlled by the Gratwick Syndicate of Buffalo, New York. The Vans were masters at getting others who had capital to invest in their plans, and so after rounding up investors the Vans approached the Buffalo firm and succeeded in gaining an option on the land. In 1906 they bought the acreage for $1 million (equivalent to about $19.5 million in 2004).

The brothers formed the Van Sweringen Company to oversee their development, and they hired the F. A. Pease Engineering Company to produce the plat map for the upscale community which they would build in the old Shaker lands. Working with the larger context of the Shaker lands meant that the Vans would be planning an entire community, not just a single boulevard. It must have excited O.P. in particular, who had a penchant for thinking big.

The brothers succeeded remarkably well at their task. Their planning was comprehensive and exacting, and Shaker Heights developed into one of the nation's earliest examples of a planned suburban community.

The Van Sweringens' concept called for a community of broad boulevards, with Shaker Boulevard as the centerpiece, and

with gracefully curving side streets, large residential lots, and land reserved for recreational and civic purposes. They established a strict zoning code, requiring that each residence be of a design distinct from every other one, and they retained a right to veto any plans that they believed would not contribute to a harmonious whole. Tudor and Georgian architectural styles were favored. The Vans specified that no home could be built for a cost less than $17,000 (an amount that today would be equivalent to about $320,000). These provisions remained in effect throughout the Vans' period of control. As a result, Shaker Heights grew into a distinctive community, gracefully laid out, and marked by homes of architectural merit.

The brothers did not want their model community to be spoiled by commercial buildings, and so at first no provisions for them had been made. The brothers recognized, however, that people wanted convenience, and out of that understanding, they later undertook the development

The stately Moreland Courts apartment complex stretched along Shaker Boulevard from Moreland Boulevard (today Van Aken Boulevard) to Coventry Road. (Blaine Hays Collection)

There was still a great
deal of open land in the
Vans' Shaker development
when in 1920 the rapid
transit line began running
directly to East 34th Street
on private right-of-way.
The scene looks southeast
from the intersection of
Shaker Boulevard and
Coventry Road.
(Blaine Hays Collection)

of the Shaker Square shopping center. Located at the western end of their development, and actually within the borders of the City of Cleveland, Shaker Square was a further sign of the brothers' forward thinking, an archtype of the suburban shopping centers of today. In it they found a harmonious way to join residential and commercial properties. The Georgian brick Shaker Square buildings would provide shopping convenience while not infringing on the character the brothers wished to maintain for their residential community.

Shaker Heights did not sprout overnight. At first, lots in the development sold rather slowly, and in 1911, when Shaker Heights was incorporated, its population stood at only 200. O.P. and M.J. recognized that a key reason for the lack of rapid growth was the absence of convenient public transportation. Once again they turned to Cleveland Railway's John Stanley, but this time they were rebuffed. Stanley explained that running

streetcars into sparsely populated areas may have been good for development, but it was not good for the transit company's bottom line. He told the brothers: get the people first, and then the streetcar line will be built.

The Vans, however, were not willing to see their plans stymied by the Railway's refusal. If the Cleveland Railway Company would not build a streetcar line for them, they would build it themselves. At the same time, the brothers were not inclined to settle for an ordinary streetcar line into their new subdivision. Standard streetcar operations were too slow. For their model city only rapid transit would do.

The brothers, of course, had already studied their options. The topography of the area clearly suggested to them that a natural ravine west of Shaker Square provided the logical setting for a rail line. The route could continue to about East 34th Street via the natural cut made by Kingsbury Run. This route would take the line to about 1.5 miles west of Public

Square. But that would not quite do, and so in 1909 the brothers bought property on the southwest quadrant of Public Square where some day they hoped to build a station for their rapid transit line. The Vans planned ahead.

It was a chance encounter with Alfred H. Smith of the New York Central Railroad (NYC) that redirected the brothers' primary attention from Shaker Heights to downtown Cleveland. The New York Central needed new downtown freight facilities, and Smith saw that the planned alignment of the Vans' rapid transit line could help him gain access to a site at Orange Avenue and East 14th Street which he wanted for a freight terminal. A deal was signed, and the New York Central ended up financing most of the Vans' transit right-of-way to downtown. The agreement would be but the first of several cooperative ventures with the railroad.

Building the rapid transit line would take time, but meanwhile the Vans were eager to spur the sluggish pace of sales on their Shaker property. So once again the Vans approached Cleveland Railway. This time they agreed to pay for construction of a branch off the Fairmount streetcar line which would run south via the Coventry Road median to Shaker Boulevard, and then east onto the Shaker center reservation to Fontenay Road. They formed the Cleveland Interurban Railroad (CIRR) as the line's owner, but since they were not yet ready to operate the line themselves, the brothers negotiated with the Cleveland Railway to be the operator. The Vans committed themselves to cover both building and operating costs. With those provisions in place, John Stanley finally agreed. The Shaker line started service on December 17, 1913. The temporary arrangement had gained a transit line for Shaker Heights,

Before Shaker Square became square and before the shopping center was built, it was known as Moreland Circle. (Cleveland *Press* Collection of the Cleveland State University Libraries)

but it was far from rapid. The circuitous route from Fontenay Road to Public Square took 55 minutes.

In order to extend the tracks for their rapid transit line from East 34th Street to Public Square, the brothers realized that they would have to get permission from the New York, Chicago, and St. Louis Railroad (better known as the Nickel Plate) to cross its existing right-of-way. At the time the Nickel Plate was a subsidiary of the larger New York Central Railroad. The courts had ordered the New York Central to divest itself of its interest in the smaller line. Alfred Smith once again entered the picture, and he persuaded the brothers to solve their access issue while at the same time helping NYC divest itself of the Nickel Plate, a 523-mile steam railroad that operated between Buffalo, New York, and Chicago. In 1916 the Vans bought the Nickel Plate Railroad for $8.5 million. They put only $2 million down (proceeds received from a bank loan), and negotiated terms of the sale so that no further payments on the purchase would be required for another five years. It was typical of the brothers' creative financing.

The Van Sweringen holdings were growing. They had started in the real estate business; to make that enterprise a success, they found themselves in the streetcar business; to bring that venture to completion, they were nudged into the railroad business. They were building an empire, and incredibly its foundation was chiefly borrowed money.

At the time they took over the Nickel Plate, it had been only marginally profitable. The Vans knew that it needed effective leadership. Besides being good salesmen, the brothers also had a good eye for capable talent. They demonstrated that skill when they lured John J. Bernet from his post with the New York Central to run their railroad. Under his leadership, the Nickel Plate was rebuilt and revitalized. It soon became a highly profitable enterprise for the Vans. (Today the Nickel Plate is part of the Norfolk Southern Railroad.)

With the right-of-way finally in their control, the Van Sweringens moved toward construction of the rapid transit route. The Vans created their own Woodhill Construction Company to build the line from Moreland Circle (the original

It has been a long tradition to light up Shaker Square for the Christmas holidays. The Vans developed Shaker Square in 1929 as a convenient shopping center for residents of Shaker Heights. (Cleveland *Press* Collection of the Cleveland State University Libraries)

name for what is now Shaker Square) to East 92nd Street. They then hired the Welsh Construction Company to build a branch line from the Circle along Moreland Boulevard (now Van Aken Boulevard) to Lynnfield Road. Welsh Construction was also commissioned to complete the right of way between East 92nd and East 34th streets. There the line would leave its private right of way, climb to the surface, and follow the existing tracks of the Cleveland Railway Company's Broadway streetcar line to a loop on Public Square. In the brothers' view, that surface diversion was only a temporary expedient, for their plans were maturing for a direct route to a station on the property they owned on Public Square.

Construction on the rapid transit line began in 1914, but then was suspended when the nation's World War I military requirements created a materials shortage. After the Armistice, work resumed, and on April 11, 1920, Shaker Heights residents were finally treated to truly rapid transit service. The previous travel time between the Shaker Heights terminal points and Public Square was cut to 33 minutes (for a complete history of the Shaker Heights Rapid Transit, — cf. Toman in the reference list).

The rapid transit route was effective in spurring sales of the Vans' Shaker properties, but they still had work to do on their idea for a downtown terminal for their line. That idea, of course, resulted in the massive Cleveland Union Terminal and the soaring Terminal Tower Building. Its story continues in Chapter Two.

But before the story shifts to the Public Square development, a brief look at the Van Sweringens' other work is in order (a wonderful telling of the entire Van Sweringen story is available — cf. Harwood in the reference list).

As the station plans were being developed, the Vans' empire continued to expand. Locally, 1929 was a particularly

The Van Sweringen brothers briefly lived in this home on South Park Boulevard, before turning it over to their sisters, Edith and Carrie. (Shaker Historical Museum)

M. J. Van Sweringen

O. P. Van Sweringen

The Cleveland *Press* of June 28, 1930, featured these drawings by editorial artist Jack Lustig, to honor the Vans on the day that their Cleveland Union Terminal project was dedicated.

busy year for the brothers. In that year they opened the Shaker Square shopping center, they purchased The Higbee Company department store, and they formed the Metropolitan Utilities Company, and through it gained control of the Cleveland Railway Company.

They also became much more involved in the railroad industry. Although frustrated in their plans by the resistance of the Interstate Commerce Commission (ICC), they had hopes of developing the fourth great railroad system in the eastern part of the United States as equals to the dominant New York Central, Pennsylvania, and Baltimore and Ohio (B&O) railroads. But although ICC approval for the fourth system was not forthcoming, the Vans assembled the pieces of a railroad empire which they believed would ultimately force the ICC to give its imprimatur to a fait accompli. They proceeded to gain control over several major railroads. Into their Allegheny Corporation holding company, they deposited among others the Toledo, St. Louis & Western (known as the Clover

Leaf route), Lake Erie and Western, Chesapeake and Ohio (affectionately known as the Chessie System), as well as the Erie, Pere Marquette, and Wheeling and Lake Erie railroads.

In 1930 they purchased their last railroad property, the Missouri Pacific, a dubious decision in the worsening days of the Depression. Altogether their railroad lines had grown to include 27,000 miles of trackage. At its peak, their vast business conglomerate, which was spread across the country, was variously estimated to have been worth $3-4 billion (over $30 billion in today's dollars). At the time, their personal fortune was calculated at $100 million ($1.3 billion today). The Vans managed the entire business from Cleveland.

The brothers' private lives gave ample evidence of their wealth. Having never married, they built a comfortable home on South Park Boulevard for themselves and their two sisters, Edith and Carrie. The South Park property remained the home for their sisters, but the brothers did not long linger there. In 1924 they moved to Daisy Hill, a 25-acre estate in Hunting Valley and into a $3 million, 54-room mansion designed by Philip Small (who together with Carl Rowley were also to be the Vans' architects for Shaker Square and most of the Moreland Courts apartment complex).

The crash of the stock market in 1929 weakened the Van's control over their holdings, but their spirit remained undaunted, as their 1930 purchase of the Missouri Pacific demonstrated. But then, as the Depression deepened, revenues from their many enterprises began to shrink. Since the brothers had built their empire through a series of heavily leveraged holding companies, the decline in revenue made servicing their corporate debt increasingly difficult. To keep their holdings intact, the brothers had no choice but to negotiate even more loans, and to accomplish this, they had to assume the new borrowings as their private debt. O.P. and M.J.'s personal obligations climbed to just under $60 million by the end of 1930.

Over the next few years the financial problems became even more acute, and the brothers devoted just about all their time in juggling one account to support another. Two local banks which had generously supported the Vans, Union Trust and Guardian Bank, went bankrupt in 1933. Much of the rest of the Vans' debt was held by New York banks, and by 1935

they decided that they could no longer put off foreclosure on the brothers' overdue accounts.

It looked as though the end had come, but then O.P found a guardian angel in local businessman George Tomlinson, president of Tomlinson Fleet Corporation, which had offices on the Terminal Tower's 29th floor. Tomlinson, in turn, invited a friend, financier George Ball of Indiana, to join ranks and bid for the Vans' properties. Forming a new company, the Mid-America Corporation, Tomlinson and Ball bid just over $3 million for a Van Sweringen empire worth a thousand times that amount. On September 30, 1935, the banks accepted the offer, writing off the rest in tax relief. Tomlinson and Ball immediately

A throng of 2,500 attended the dedicatory ceremonies for the Cleveland Union Terminal. The reclusive Van Sweringen brothers, however, chose not to be present. (Cleveland *Press* Collection of the Cleveland State University Libraries)

The Vans, O. P. (left) and M. J. (right), during their struggle to preserve the empire they had built. (Cleveland Picture Collection of Cleveland Public Library)

hired the Van Sweringens to manage their Mid-America Corporation. The two brothers were once again in charge of the empire they had built, and now had the added benefit of new executive salaries. On top of their salaries, the brothers received a stock option which over the next ten years would allow them to buy controlling interest in the new company, which would make them once again not only managers but owners as well.

With the Mid-America bailout, it seemed that O.P. and M.J. had weathered the worst and once again were on their way to the top. But it was not to be. The relentless pressures they had faced since 1930 had taken a physical toll. M. J., the younger brother, suffered from high blood pressure, and he was exhausted by the five-year financial ordeal. Further weakened by an attack of influenza, his condition deteriorated. He died in Lakeside Hospital on December 13, 1935, aged 54. His brother O.P. was at his side.

M.J.'s death must have been devastating for O.P.. Throughout their lives, the brothers had been largely inseparable, even sharing an office when at work and a bedroom when at Daisy Hill. Nonetheless, O.P. carried on his duties as chief executive for Mid-America Corporation. On one of his business missions to New York City, the 57-year-old O.P. suffered a heart attack and died within minutes of the train's arrival in Hoboken. He had survived his brother by less than a year.

Those who knew the brothers well mourned their passing. Others, though, who had paid a financial price for having invested too heavily in the brothers' great dreams, did not share in the grief. They blamed the Vans' for what they thought had been a reckless way of building their business pyramid.

Regardless of the judgments that history has made of the Van Sweringens' financial methods, no one can ignore their achievements. In the lasting distinction of their suburban real estate developments and in their transformation of the center of downtown Cleveland, the brothers' legacy continues to loom large indeed.

In large part because of the brothers' vision and the dramatic impact which their terminal project achieved, Cleveland erased its small-town image and assumed the appearance of a major American city.

For 75 years, the soaring Terminal Tower and its integrated components have proudly stood as the City of Cleveland's chief symbol. The Tower also stands as a vivid memorial to a spirit which would not think in small terms and through which an ordinary city rose to greatness.

Despite their great achievements, few actual memorials to the Van Sweringens exist. This plaque was placed in the restored Midland Arcade, renamed the Van Sweringen Arcade in 1986 to honor the two brothers – note the misspelling of "Oris." (Landmark Office Towers Collection)

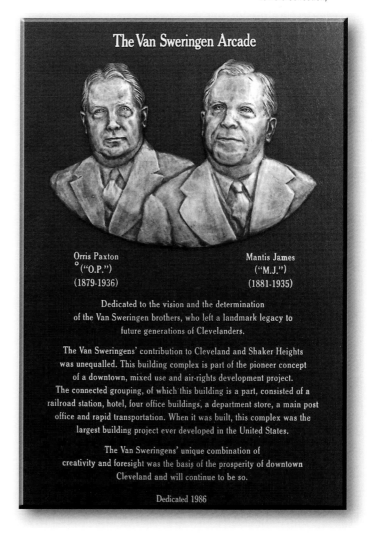

The Van Sweringen Arcade

Orris Paxton
°("O.P.")
(1879-1936)

Mantis James
("M.J.")
(1881-1935)

Dedicated to the vision and the determination of the Van Sweringen brothers, who left a landmark legacy to future generations of Clevelanders.

The Van Sweringens' contribution to Cleveland and Shaker Heights was unequalled. This building complex is part of the pioneer concept of a downtown, mixed use and air-rights development project. The connected grouping, of which this building is a part, consisted of a railroad station, hotel, four office buildings, a department store, a main post office and rapid transportation. When it was built, this complex was the largest building project ever developed in the United States.

The Van Sweringens' unique combination of creativity and foresight was the basis of the prosperity of downtown Cleveland and will continue to be so.

Dedicated 1986

The Face of the City is Changed

chapter 2

When in 1909 the Van Sweringen brothers purchased some property edging the southwest quadrant of Public Square, their intent was modest. They needed a terminal for the rapid transit line they hoped to build between their Shaker Heights development and Cleveland's central business district. Like all Van Sweringen plans, however, their idea for an interurban station was destined to grow. Over the next decade, their original thinking was transformed into the most ambitious building project ever undertaken in Cleveland.

At the time the Vans first thought of a downtown interurban station, the city was served by several of these intercity streetcar lines. The Cleveland, Painesville & Eastern, the Eastern Ohio Traction, and the Northern Ohio Traction & Light served areas to the east and southeast of downtown Cleveland. The Lake Shore Electric and the Cleveland Southwestern connected Cleveland with areas to the west and southwest. Together with their own Cleveland Interurban Railroad, the Vans believed that a downtown facility

which could serve all six lines would make good transportation sense and be financially supportable.

At the time the city was also served by several steam passenger railroads. It had intercity service from the Pennsylvania; New York Central; Cleveland, Cincinnati, Chicago and St. Louis (known as the Big Four and operated as a subsidiary of the New York Central); Wheeling and Lake

In 1900 the southwest quadrant of Public Square bore a rustic look. It featured a lagoon and a pedestrian bridge. Just visible to the right is the Forest City House hotel. (Cleveland Picture Collection of Cleveland Public Library)

During its dedication on November 10, 1865, the Union Depot was hailed as "a monument to the progressive spirit of Cleveland. It will stand through the ages. Time will not affect its stone and iron." Those were proud words, but they were certainly not prophetic. By the turn of the century, the depot was congested, battered, and dirty. Most visitors to Cleveland came via the Pennsylvania and NYC railroads, and the dismal station that greeted them upon arrival utterly failed to convey the kind of impression coveted by Cleveland's city fathers. By 1912, however, plans were finally getting underway to correct that situation.

A new lakefront station was originally conceived as part of what has come to be known as Cleveland's Group Plan. The brainchild of one of Cleveland's greatest mayors, Tom L. Johnson (1901-1909), the Group Plan was the work of a commission composed of Daniel H. Burnham, Arnold R. Brunner, and John M. Carerre. Their recommended Group Plan was revealed in 1903. It called for clearing 101 acres of land between West Third and East Ninth streets from Lakeside Avenue south to Superior Avenue. At the time, the area was occupied by a collection of aging private homes and commercial buildings. In their place would rise a grouping of civic buildings united in architectural idiom. These were to be connected by a large open expanse of green, known as the Mall. At the northern end of the Mall would be a new railroad station.

Erie; Baltimore and Ohio; Erie; and Nickel Plate railroads. The Wheeling and Lake Erie station was on Ontario Street, the Nickel Plate station was at Broadway and East Ninth Street, while the B&O and the Erie had their stations in the flats. The New York Central and the Pennsylvania shared the decrepit Union Depot on the lakefront at West Ninth Street.

The first of the Group Plan buildings to be completed was the U.S. Post Office, Customs House and Court House Building adjacent to the northeast quadrant of Public Square. (Cleveland Picture Collection of Cleveland Public Library)

The first of the Group Plan buildings to be completed was the U.S. Post Office, Customs House and Court House Building (today usually referred to as the old

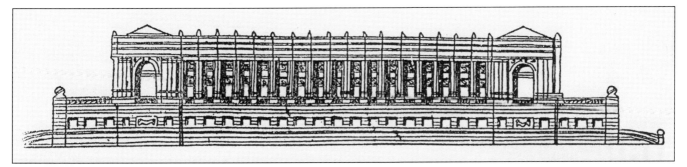

Federal Building). It opened in 1911 at the corner of Superior Avenue and Public Square. Other buildings in the plan followed: the Cuyahoga County Court House (1912) and Cleveland City Hall (1916) on Lakeside Avenue, the Public Auditorium (1922) and Cleveland Board of Education Building (1930) along East Sixth Street, and the main Cleveland Public Library Building (1925) on Superior Avenue.

The new union station, however, remained in limbo, delayed by a dispute between the city and the railroads over ownership of several acres of lakefront land. In 1907 the B&O and the Erie railroads had expressed some interest in a new station facility adjacent to the southwest quadrant of Public Square. Entering the city from the south, the B&O and Erie did not find the idea of a lakefront station appealing. But the city fathers were committed to the lakefront site, and the B&O/Erie proposal faded away.

Then in a 1915 Union Depot ordinance, the city and the Pennsylvania and New York Central railroads reached an agreement on the lakefront land issue. It looked as though the lakefront station project would finally move forward.

It was about that time that the Van Sweringen brothers revived the idea of a station at Public Square, one which would serve both the interurban lines

and the steam railroads. To carry forward their plan, the brothers announced formation of a series of companies under whose direction their plan would be carried forward. These included the Cleveland Union Terminals Company to build the railroad portion of their plan, a Cleveland Traction Terminals Company to take care of the needs of the interurbans and to operate the stores they planned for the station, and a Cleveland Terminals Building Company to control the development of buildings that would rise on air rights over the station property. Engineering plans for the development were completed in 1918. It all sounded quite impressive.

But the Vans could not proceed until a final decision was made about the site for

The proponents for a new lakefront railroad station commissioned this drawing of the facility which they hoped to see located at the foot of Mall C.
(Cleveland *Press* photo, Cleveland Landmarks Press Collection)

The Van Sweringens countered the Mall station proponents by releasing this picture of their proposed union station at Public Square.
(Cleveland Union Terminal Archives of the Cleveland State University Libraries)

the new station. The city couldn't support stations at both the lakefront and Public Square locations, and the final decision about location had not been made. Soon factions dedicated to both plans were engaged in battle. The dispute, which at times became bitter, dragged on for almost three years, until Cleveland voters finally settled the matter on January 6, 1919. In a special election that day, they approved the Ordinance of 1919, which authorized the Public Square site for the new station. The vote was 30,758 in favor to 19,916 opposed.

The ordinance cleared the way for the Terminal Group project. It set forth a multitude of details about site development, the construction process, and the eventual upkeep of the facility.

Work on the Terminal project actually began in 1920. Clearing the land downtown got underway two years later. Some 1,400 buildings were razed on about 35 acres of land, stretching from Superior Avenue and Public Square to the north, Ontario Street to the East, West Ninth Street to the west, and to Canal Street to the south, just above the meandering route of the Cuyahoga River. Several roadways were vacated for the project, the best known of which were Champlain and Michigan streets. The wreckers' ball brought down many familiar buildings, but it also rid the city of some deteriorated structures and slum dwellings. The dedication book for the new facility, *The Union Station*, described the area in these words:

In 1923 streetcars continued to loop around Public Square, but most of the buildings that had lined the Ontario Street site for the Terminal Complex had been razed. (Bruce Young Collection)

"a hodge-podge of 'one-flight-up' shops, 'hot dog' stands, and popcorn cubbyholes. The improvements not only obliterated these shacks, but also the block after block of adjoining rookeries that so stubbornly resisted the march of modern business and civic progress."

While the construction work downtown was the most dramatic, the actual boundaries of the Terminal project extended well beyond. The Cleveland Union Terminal section of the railroad right-of-way stretched from East 40th Street to West 37th Street where the Nickel Plate connected to the CUT trackage. From those points work was also required on the New York Central right-of-way to Collinwood and the Big Four right-of-way to Linndale, a stretch of 17 miles. This area of track was to be served by electric locomotives, and so catenary towers and overhead power lines dotted the landscape. New suburban

passenger stations were erected in both Linndale and East Cleveland. The most dramatic part of providing access to the downtown station site was from the west. It involved building a 3,450-foot viaduct over the Flats and the Cuyahoga River. Along the right-of-way from East 34th

Bridges were a key part of the Terminal construction project. The bridge structure for the Prospect Avenue extension is at the left. (Cleveland *Press* photo, Cleveland Landmarks Press Collection)

The Cleveland Union Terminal Viaduct is nearing completion in 1929. It brought trains from the west to the station. (Cleveland Union Terminal Archives of the Cleveland State University Libraries)

Street and Pittsburgh Avenue to downtown, retaining walls protected the new rail alignment from any collapse of the steep hillsides that lined the northern edge of the right-of-way. A total of 22 new bridges were needed to segregate the railroad alignment. A freight line branched from the mainline tracks to a large new Northern Ohio Food Terminal at East 37th Street and Orange Avenue.

The main focus, of course, was at the downtown site. A gaping hole appeared where the grimy collection of buildings had stood, and work was underway to lay out the track area for the new station and to lay the foundation needed to support the tall buildings which would be built above the station and its right-of-way. At the downtown site, five bridges were built to carry roadways over the Union Station site. These included Prospect Avenue, Huron Road, and West Second, Third, and Sixth

streets. The Prospect and Huron bridges connected Ontario Street on the east to Superior Avenue on the west, and the other three ran between Huron and Ontario.

The Van Sweringen plan encompassed much more than the railroad/interurban station. The entire project was to be an interconnected complex comprising a hotel (which was actually completed before the other construction got underway), a department store, a new postal facility, and seven office buildings.

As the Depression came on and the Van Sweringen fortune disappeared, the plan was not fully developed. What was built resulted in some five million square feet of space, but that amounted to only about 45% of what had been envisioned. Construction came to a halt in 1934 with the completion of the U.S. Post Office Building (now the MK-Ferguson Plaza). Various gaps remained along the complex's perimeter: at the corner of Prospect Avenue and Huron Road; adjacent to the station's skylight structure between West Second and West Third streets; west of the Post Office building in a triangle bounded by Huron Road, Superior Avenue and West Sixth Street; and on Superior Avenue, west of the Hotel Cleveland building.

It took 32 years to close the first of those gaps, when a banquet hall was built for the Hotel Cleveland. Then came the Lausche State Office Building in the triangle formed by the Huron Road and West Sixth Street bridges where they meet Superior Avenue. That came about in 1979. Another gap was

closed in 1990 by the Skylight Office Tower and Ritz Carlton Hotel/Chase Financial Tower (originally Chemical Financial Tower) buildings, erected as part of the Tower City Center project. The other gaps, however, still remain.

It was not the empty places, though, that the community focused on in 1930 when the still unfinished complex was dedicated.

On a cool Saturday, June 28, 1930, the Cleveland Chamber of Commerce hosted a giant reception for some 2,500 civic leaders in the Union Terminal's main concourse. The guest list comprised Cleveland Who's Who of the day, Ohio's two United

Looking west, the tracks lead to the new Cleveland Union Terminal Viaduct. At the left is the B&O station. To the right is the Erie station and the Detroit-Superior Bridge. (Herbert H. Harwood Collection)

The track work on the east side was complex. To the right is the Northern Ohio food Terminal. Beyond it, towards the top of the picture, is the New York Central freight station, and beyond that the Nickel Plate facilities. The electrified main line winds through the center of the scene. (Robert Runyon photo, Cleveland Landmarks Press Collection)

States senators, Cleveland Mayor John D. Marshall, and executives from the passenger railroads which served the city. President Herbert Hoover sent a congratulatory letter which was read to the assembly. William Ganson Rose, noted civic leader and historian, served as master of ceremonies.

Notable, however, for their absence from the celebration were the two men who made it all happen, the Van Sweringen brothers. Perhaps it was because they were reclusive by nature. Or perhaps it was because they sensed that the deepening Depression allowed no time for celebration.

As part of the community's salute to the newly-completed Terminal project, the Cleveland *Plain Dealer* published a special section in its Sunday, June 29, 1930, edition devoted to the Union Terminal development. Echoing sentiments that resounded during the previous day's dedication ceremonies, the paper stated, "It is no wild guess to predict that buildings will still be erected on property owned by the Van Sweringen Corporation twenty-five years hence."

The editorial, of course, missed the mark. The Vans and their corporate identity disappeared early. And for more than 25 years, there were no major changes to the property. But eventually change and development did come. The most recent addition is the Carl B. Stokes Federal Courthouse. The Depression had stalled further development to the Vans' great achievement, but it did not end it.

While the Vans' entire dream for the site was not completed during their lifetimes, what was accomplished during those first 14 years of development on the Public Square site changed the face of the city and gave Clevelanders much to be proud of. The massive Terminal Complex was novel in conception and grand in scope.

It was also expensive. The final bill for the project amounted to $179 million. If that cost were converted into 2004 dollars, the price tag would soar to nearly $1.84 billion, eclipsing by a large margin any other project ever undertaken in Cleveland.

The Terminal Complex's physical dimensions were monumental, but the project also stands as a monument in another way. For 75 years it has stood as a symbol of the kind of adventurous spirit that was a hallmark of the City of Cleveland during the first third of the Twentieth Century, a spirit uniquely personified by the two brothers who built it. The Terminal Complex also serves as a reminder to all Clevelanders that the future well-being of their city depends on great vision: to once again dare to dream great plans and to focus the will of civic

This view of the Terminal Tower Complex reveals some of the unfinished pieces in the development. One site is at bottom left, next to the Hotel Cleveland; to the right, another surrounds the clerestory building of the Union Station, between the Post Office and Midland buildings. (Bruce Young Collection)

The brick surface of the Builders Exchange/Guildhall Building was meant to be temporary. Another office tower was to have occupied the location. (J. A. Toman photo)

leaders (with the whole community in chorus) to provide the leadership and resources to make them come true.

Perhaps the Dedication Day editorial in The Cleveland *Press* said it best: "A city writes its epics not in words, but in stone and steel." Comparing the new station to the old Union Depot, it went on that "we offer this contrast between 1865 and 1930 as a token of what fruits we have cultured on the soil it

bequeathed us." The editorial rightly assessed the contrast. For 75 years the Terminal Complex has been the epic center for Clevelanders. It has stood the test of time, and though challenged by cultural, economic, and transportation changes, the Complex has not only survived them, but more importantly, it has triumphed over them.

An historical tour of the various components in the complex follows.

The open triangle between Huron Road and Superior Avenue reveals another of the gaps in the project. It was filled in 1979 by construction of a new State of Ohio office building. (Cleveland Landmarks Press Collection)

The Van Sweringen Terminal project changed the face of the city. The view shows the complex as it looked from 1934 until 1979. (Bruce Young Collection)

This view from the Terminal Tower shows the 1979 Lausche State Office Building (left) and the Rockefeller Building; these two frame the western entry into downtown. (Jack Muslovski photo)

Union Station
to the Avenue

chapter 3

The Avenue at Tower City Center is a busy place. It daily draws tens of thousands of people to its stores, restaurants, and food court, to the Regional Transit Authority rapid transit station, or to the different passageways that lead to the Landmark Office Towers, Gund Arena, or the Carl B. Stokes Federal Courthouse. Some will pause to enjoy the fountains or to gaze up through the skylights. Few, however, will detect much evidence of the original purpose of this vast and busy space. Between 1988 and 1990, as the major renovation which resulted in creating The Avenue was underway, the most obvious markers of the space's history were either totally removed or creatively readapted to new purposes.

The Avenue at Tower City Center occupies the space that was once Cleveland Union Terminal. Over the years hundreds of thousands of people made their way to and from the station, maneuvering the staircases to and from the railroad passenger platforms. It was where thousands more eagerly awaited their visitors or bade farewell to loved ones setting out on treks

Work on the Terminal Tower Building is far along, but the site for the new station is just being cleared, 1926. (Cleveland Picture Collection of Cleveland Public Library)

across the country. The hum of a thousand conversations blended with the rumble of arriving trains, the echoing sound of the public address system announcing imminent departures on track such-and-such, and the familiar call of "all aboard." Cleveland Union Terminal was created as a palace worthy of the passenger train which was then the undisputed king of intercity travel.

While the first sketches for Cleveland's union station showed it following in the footsteps of the Grand Central Station, with a large and imposing edifice rising above track level, a concept common in most major cities, the plans soon changed. Cleveland's new union station was to be built below ground level. The air rights

41

In this scene from the west, construction activity is brisk as the track system for the new Cleveland Union Station is laid into place, November 1929. (Herbert H. Harwood Collection)

Track work is just about complete, three months before the first passenger train will enter the new Cleveland Union Station, February 1930. Construction continues on the Midland Building in the background. (Herbert H. Harwood Collection)

above it were to be developed into major office and commercial space. With the exception of the clerestory for the station's main concourse, which stood south of Prospect Avenue between West Second and West Third streets, there would be no hint at surface level that a great railroad facility existed.

The initial plan for the station had envisioned a stub-end terminal with two levels of tracks below the street, the lowest for the interurban lines and the one above it for the steam passenger lines. That concept

soon changed. The new plan called for a through-terminal layout, with the train and interurban tracks laid out side by side on a single below-ground level.

The key concept for Cleveland's new station, "air rights," itself was not new. It had been developed by William Wilgus, the New York Central Railroad's chief engineer for building the Grand Central Terminal in New York City. He realized that using clean electrically powered locomotives instead of smoke-producing steam engines meant that the railroad's approach tracks and storage yards could be safely buried in tunnels below street level. This choice of motive power allowed the New York Central Railroad to enter the real estate business, developing high rise office towers, hotels, and apartment buildings above the buried track system leading to the station. The Cleveland plan utilized the concept Wilgus so successfully implemented in New York City, but whereas New York's Grand Central Station itself is a monumental above-ground building, in Cleveland even the station would be located below ground level.

Architect for the Cleveland Union Terminal was the Chicago firm of Graham, Anderson, Probst & White. The firm was an amalgamation of partnerships with a distinguished past. Part of its heritage could be found in the Graham, Burnham Company of Chicago, which had emerged from the Burnham and Root Company. The latter had designed Cleveland's first high-rise office structure, the Society for Savings Building on the northeast quadrant of Public Square, and Daniel Burnham himself had served on the city's Group Plan Commission. The firm could also

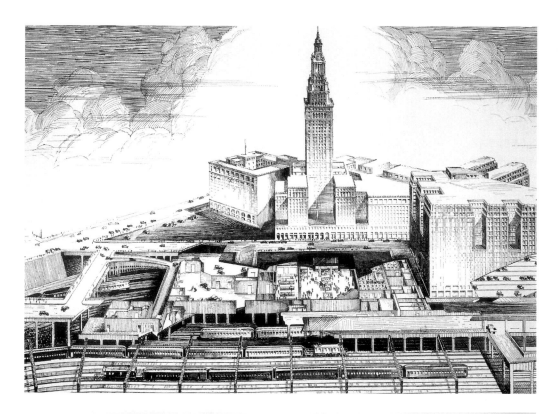

This architectural drawing illustrates the use of air-rights in the CUT design. Track and Concourse levels are below street level. (Richard E. Karberg Collection)

CUT is in full operation in June 1930. The coach yard tracks are to the right; the tracks to the passenger platforms can be seen curving below West Sixth Street through the gap where the U. S. Post Office Building will soon be under construction. (Herbert H. Harwood Collection)

The clerestory building, which housed the superstructure for the skylight over the Steam Concourse, is the only part of the station that rose above street level. (Jack Muslovski photograph, Cleveland Landmarks Press Collection)

trace part of its history to the New York City partnership of McKim, Meade and White. That firm had been responsible for the Hanna mansion in Bratenahl and more recently had designed the New York Municipal Building. The Van Sweringens hired Henry D. Jouett from the New York Central to be chief engineer for the project, and the New York firm of Aronberg, Fried & Company as the general contractor.

Construction on the station proper began in May 1928. The Cleveland Union Terminals Company, which was responsible for building the station and then for operating it, was a typical Van Sweringen creation. It was financed, and therefore

CUT had a fleet of 22 electric locomotives to bring trains into the station. This engine bears its original number, 1058. Later the fleet was renumbered 200-221. (Cleveland Union Terminal Archives of the Cleveland State University Libraries)

actually owned, by the New York Central Railroad, whose share of the project gave it a 93% ownership, and by the Nickel Plate Railroad, which owned the remaining 7%. The Vans, as usual, had negotiated their own control over the company. After the Vans were gone from the scene, the railroads both owned and managed the facility until it was finally sold in 1980.

The original plans of the Van Sweringen brothers, to build a station for their rapid transit lines, had long since been revised. The facility under construction was to be truly a "union" station, one which the brothers hoped would serve all of the steam railroads and interurban lines entering the city, as well as the new rapid transit lines they planned to build.

The Union Terminal plans were drawn to allow future expansion, but that contingency did not materialize. By 1928 the city's interurban network had already been cut in half. The Pennsylvania Railroad had refused to have anything to do with the new facility. It was content to continue using the old Union Depot on the lakefront (that facility continued serving the Pennsy until September 27, 1953) as well as its other station at Euclid Avenue and East 55th Street. Although the Wheeling and Lake Erie station had been declared unsafe and was demolished in 1929, that railroad chose to move into the Erie station rather than commit to the Union Terminal.

At the time, steam was still the main source of motive power for the railroads, but the Van Sweringen brothers did not want the dirt from steam locomotives to pollute their new station nor their noise to disturb the tenants in the office towers above. As a result, they provided for transfer points to the east and west of downtown where trains would exchange their steam engines for electric locomotives for a quiet and clean ride to the new terminal. While the choice was environmentally friendly, it was also costly, a factor which played a key role in the decision of the Pennsylvania and the other railroads to opt out of using CUT.

To accommodate the electrification plan, catenary and overhead wiring was put into place along 17 miles of track between Collinwood and Linndale. The Cleveland Electric Illuminating Company provided the power at 11,000 volts of alternating current. This was delivered to two substations, located near the eastern and western ends of the electrified trackage, where it was converted to 3,000 volts direct current.

To bring the trains into the new facility, 22 powerful electric locomotives were purchased from the General Electric Company. These huge locomotives measured 80 feet in length, and were capable of speeds up to 70 miles per hour.

Construction work proceeded at a brisk pace, and by 1930 the huge new station was ready to receive its first passengers. Cleveland Union Terminal boasted 734,000 square feet of space on its several levels.

Track level was the lowest. Plans originally provided for a total of 34 tracks, ten for rapid transit use and 24 for the passenger railroads. The changing rail scene, however, resulted in a decision that fewer tracks would do the job. As a result, only six tracks were installed for rapid transit use (tracks 2-7). Track 1, which had been intended for use by interurbans arriving from the west, was not built.

The traction tracks were located in the northern end of the station.

South of the rapid transit tracks were 12 tracks for passenger train service, and one more which served as a running track through the station yard (tracks 11-23). Nine additional tracks stretched across the southernmost part of the facility. These served as a coach yard; in the original plan, they had been reserved to serve additional passenger platforms should the need arise. Movement in and out of the new terminal was controlled from a Signal Building located just east of the coach

This view shows the eastern rail approach to the station under construction. Work is underway on the rapid transit tracks which will use the set of tunnels at the right to enter the station. (Bruce Young Collection)

Cleveland Union Station is in its first month of operation. The view is toward the east. The tracks are leading to the passenger platforms. There were six platforms, each serving two tracks. (Cleveland *Press* photos, Cleveland Landmarks Press Collection)

The Van Sweringens' dedication booklet for the new station offered this drawing of what the main passenger concourse would look like. (*The Union Station*)

yard. It boasted the largest interlocking switching machine in the world.

Passenger platforms of varying lengths were situated between every two sets of tracks. The shortest of the platforms, 261 feet in length, was for rapid transit use. The longest, 1,511 feet, was for passenger train service.

Six sets of stairways connected the steam passenger platforms to the concourse level above. Another three stairways were in place to serve passengers from the Van Sweringens' CIRR rapid transit line to Shaker Heights. Freight elevators were used to move baggage, freight, and mail from track level to their respective handling areas on the concourse level.

The concourse level of Cleveland Union Terminal was divided into three main sections. The central space was called the Main Concourse, although it was popularly known as the Steam Concourse. This huge chamber measured 238 feet in length, 120 feet in width, and had a ceiling height of 42 feet. A skylight, in the center of the ceiling, flooded the interior with natural light. Eight huge bronze chandeliers bordered the skylight.

The walls of the Steam Concourse were paneled in Botticino marble. The perimeter of the chamber was marked by 22 Doric columns, 25 feet in height, which added to the stately atmosphere of the room.

Adjoining the concourse's west wall was a spacious waiting room, with restroom facilities for women. It measured 162 feet long, 56 feet across, and 20 feet in height. It could accommodate 500 people.

To the chamber's east was the Lunch Room, which offered both table and counter service. This large room was

Passengers in the Steam Concourse await the "Now Boarding" call for New York Central's Interstate Express to Painesville, Erie, and points east. (Bruce Young Collection)

designed to handle as many as 6,000 customers during the lunch period. To the left of the Lunch Room entrance was the train board, which listed the times for arriving and departing trains. To the right was an entranceway leading to a barbershop and men's restroom.

The Steam Concourse itself was furnished with heavy wooden benches for those awaiting arrivals or departures. Its center portion was punctuated by the six stairways leading to the track level.

A wall at the southern end of the Steam Concourse separated the passenger areas from a busy vehicle passageway which connected the adjoining service areas. In 1941 the south wall was spruced up by a gift from the Cleveland Chamber of Commerce (predecessor of today's Greater Cleveland Partnership). The chamber donated a 72-foot-long porcelain enamel mural by artist J. Scott Williams. Titled *Man's Conquest of the Elemental Forces of Nature*, the mural weighed ten tons and was composed of

This porcelain-enamel mural graced the south wall of the Steam Concourse from 1941 until 1978. It is now housed at the Western Reserve Historical Society. (Cleveland Landmarks Press Collection)

300 separate pieces. Created in Cleveland at the Ferro Enamel Corporation, it had been exhibited at the New York World's Fair in 1939. The Chamber of Commerce felt that the mural should be returned to its city of origin. For the CUT installation, a "Welcome to Cleveland" panel was added below the mural. The mural is now displayed at the Western Reserve Historical Society museum.

Adjoining the Steam Concourse at its northern end (towards Public Square), was an east-west passageway, which connected the Main Concourse to the East and West Traction concourses. The lower ceiling of

A Cleveland Interurban Railroad rapid transit car speeds toward CUT. Contrary to customary practice, its westbound track is to the right of the east-bound track, an arrangement that lasted from 1930 until 1990. A passenger train heads east. (Cleveland Landmarks Press Collection)

and baggage handling. The large area devoted to these services was located at the southern end of the terminal, in an area practically unknown to the general public.

At the east end of the passageway was CUT's most elegant dining space, the English Oak Room. Designed by Philip Small, the room was beautifully paneled in English oak. Its central space was defined by gracefully carved pillars with inlaid ebony, maple, and rosewood. Its ornamental-plaster ceiling was delicately painted. Everything about the room was meant to appeal to those who chose to dine in style and comfort. The English Oak Room's furniture was the work of one of the city's foremost interior designers, Louis Rorimer. Its cuisine was excellent and its service impeccable. The English Oak Room did not just cater to the traveler. Its fine atmosphere and distinguished menu quickly made it a favorite among the city's diners.

this passageway was an indicator that it was situated beneath the bridgework that carried Prospect Avenue over the complex. The passage joined the Steam Concourse to the traction concourses and led to a taxi stand at its west end and to the English Oak Room restaurant at the east end.

The indoor cab stand was a welcome convenience. Alighting from their trains, passengers did not have to risk possible inclement weather to hail a cab. Cabs reached the stand via a ramp from West Sixth Street. This same roadway also served the areas devoted to mail express

North of the passageway was the ticket lobby, a room measuring 138 feet by 92 feet. Ticket booths lined its western wall and shops its eastern wall.

The English Oak Room was CUT's most elegant setting. Operated by the Fred Harvey chain, it was one of the city's favorite dining rooms. (Richard E. Karberg Collection)

At the northern end of the Ticket Lobby was another east-west passage, which was called the Vestibule. It too connected with the two traction concourses. From the vestibule two ramps led up to the Portico, the station's formal entrance lobby, at Public Square level. At the eastern end of the Vestibule a short ramp led to the basement level of the Higbee Department Store and to a below-ground corridor which connected Union Terminal with the three Van Sweringen office buildings located on Prospect Avenue.

To either side of CUT's central concourse area were the East and West Traction concourses. These smaller concourses were designed to accommodate passengers for the interuban and rapid transit lines. A ramp connected each traction concourse to Public Square level. Four stairways in the East Traction Concourse led to track level. The Western concourse did not have the stairways, since that space was intended for future rapid transit developments. Shops lined the walls of both concourses.

The original Van Sweringen plan envisioned a day when rapid transit lines would radiate out from the station to all parts of the city. As it turned out, for the first 25 years of the station, only the East Traction Concourse served its intended transportation purpose. The Van Sweringens' Cleveland Interurban Railroad traveled along its new right-of-way from East 34th Street to Union Terminal for the first time on July 20, 1930. That inaugural trip came 17 years after the first cars had begun service along Shaker Boulevard and over its original circuitous route from the suburb to downtown. Shaker Heights residents had finally gained an express route all the way to the heart of downtown Cleveland.

The Van Sweringens designed their union station to meet all the needs of the traveling public, and hence they had set aside 175,000 square feet of space for shops and restaurants. The Vans wanted to secure Fred Harvey, Inc., as the primary tenant for the space. Harvey's was well known for high quality service to the

CUT electric locomotive 207 has just been coupled to an east-bound train at Linndale Station. It will bring the train to the downtown station. (Herbert H. Harwood Collection)

49

The Fred Harvey soda fountain on CUT Concourse level was a great setting for a short rest stop. (Cleveland Union Terminal Archives of the Cleveland State University Libraries)

The Fred Harvey shops provided a broad array of merchandise, making them popular with both travelers and local shoppers. (Cleveland Union Terminal Archives of the Cleveland State University Libraries)

Besides the elegant English Oak Room, the Meeting Place at the station's northern end, the Tea Room at the Public Square level, and the Lunch Room, Harvey's operated a wide variety of shops in the station. Among these were a drug store, both men's and women's clothing shops, a book store, a toy store, a bakery, candy shops, a soda fountain, and news stands.

On October 23, 1929, while work on the station was nearing completion, the first passenger train glided into the new facility. The train was a special run to test the station's clearances. It must have given its two chief passengers, Oris Paxton and Mantis James Van Sweringen, great satisfaction to experience first hand the results of 20 years of planning and building.

Regular passenger service began seven months later. The first scheduled passenger train, a New York Central local from Norwalk, Ohio, pulled into the gleaming new station on May 19, 1930, inaugurating a new era in Cleveland's railroad history. While the event was celebrated by a great deal of civic hoopla, it was not quite the triumph that it might have been.

When passenger service to CUT began, only three railroads had committed to using the new station: the New York Central, its subsidiary Big Four Railroad, and the Vans' own Nickel Plate. The Pennsylvania and the Wheeling and Lake Erie had rejected the new station, and the B&O and the Erie were not yet ready to sign on. The B&O began using CUT in 1934, but the Erie did not join until 1949. The price exacted by the Erie to join CUT was that it be allowed to use diesel locomotives to pull its trains directly into the station. By 1949 CUT was so concerned about

railroading public. The "Harvey Girls" serving staff, with their perfect manners and their attractive uniforms, added to the chain's smart appeal. The Harvey chain, however, was primarily situated in the west and southwest. Chicago, its headquarters, was its most eastern operation. As Cleveland reporter Philip Porter reflected, "It was quite a coup to get the Harvey operation into Cleveland." The Van Sweringens were interested in the best, and in the Harvey chain, that is what they secured.

meeting costs that it conceded to the Erie's demand.

By 1930 railroad passenger business nationwide was already past its peak and had begun a gradual decline. When the Union Terminal opened, some 80 passenger trains were scheduled in and out of the city each day, although not all used CUT. In the city's busiest year, there had been 94 intercity passenger runs.

By the end of World War II, the number of trains had dropped to 49, and as the traveling public increasingly turned to the airlines or to their own automobiles, the number steadily declined. As the numbers dropped, the Cleveland Union Terminals Company, a subsidiary of the New York Central and Nickel Plate Railroads, began considering ways to cut costs.

In 1952, however, the company did make a modest investment in the station. For years the public had clamored for escalators to replace the stairways to track level. Finally bowing to the pressure, the railroad management installed two

escalators. These served only two platforms and only operated upward. The officials apparently felt that it was not as difficult to carry baggage down the stairways as it was to lug it up.

A major cost-cutting decision came in 1953. With the advent of the relatively clean and quiet diesel locomotive, the

Steam engines did not ordinarily make their way into CUT. This New York Central Niagara, however, was on a test run to check out catenary clearance. (Jay Himes Collection)

Diesels took over the passenger service through CUT once electrification ended in 1953. Here a New York Central train heads west on the Viaduct in December 1954. (Herbert H. Harwood photo)

Nickel Plate Train 8 is inbound
on the Viaduct, May 1956.
(Herbert H. Harwood photo)

Nickel Plate Train 8 is inbound on the Viaduct, May 1956. (Herbert H. Harwood photo)

rationale of having electric engines bring trains into the Terminal no longer served its original purpose. The expense of maintaining the overhead, the fleet of electric locomotives, the power stations, and the salaries for the extra crews involved in switching engines had become prohibitive. CUT officials decided to abandon the electrification. The last Cleveland run for the mighty electric locomotives came on November 16, 1953. They were then sent to New York City where they operated out of Grand Central Station. A remnant of the former electric days can still be seen from the rapid transit right-of-way; while the tracks, signals, and the overhead wires are long gone, many of the catenary towers remain, a rusting reminder of the electric years.

Passenger train service continued to decline. In 1960 four railroads were still utilizing the station, but their days were numbered. The last B&O passenger train to use CUT was January 4, 1963. The Nickel Plate lasted a little longer. In 1964 the Nickel Plate was absorbed by the Norfolk and Western (N&W), and the last N&W train left the terminal on September 10, 1965. That left just two railroads using CUT.

In 1968 the New York Central and the Pennsylvania railroads merged to form the ill-fated Penn Central. The consolidated railroad was still operating seven daily trains from CUT: two to Chicago, three to New York City, one to Indianapolis, and one to Columbus. The other railroad was the Erie-Lackawanna. In 1960 the Erie Railroad had merged with the Delaware, Lackawanna & Western to form the Erie-Lackawanna. That railroad had one scheduled CUT run, a commuter train between Cleveland and Youngstown, Ohio.

The Penn-Central, which as a result of the merger had become the owner of Cleveland Union Terminals Company, did not prosper. In serious financial trouble, the railroad petitioned the Interstate Commerce Commission to abandon pas-

senger operations. Permission was withheld, however, until federal legislation finally created the Amtrak rail system in 1971. Only then was Penn-Central permitted to quit the passenger business. Its last train left Cleveland Union Terminal on April 30, 1971.

The new Amtrak system did not originally have Cleveland on its route map, but after much lobbying by local officials and railfans, Amtrak in 1975 finally agreed to restore passenger train service to Cleveland. The new train was the Lake Shore Limited, with connections to

The Cleveland Transit System began its rapid transit operations in 1955. Here one of the original "bluebird" cars traverses the Viaduct. (J. William Vigrass photo)

In 1970 work has begun in converting the old coach yards into an automobile parking lot. (Cleveland *Press* Collection of the Cleveland State University Libraries)

Chain-link fences enclosed two tennis courts in the Main Concourse, a fortunately short-lived experiment. (Cleveland *Press* Collection of the Cleveland State University Libraries)

Paint peeling from the Main Concourse ceiling was only one symptom of CUT's deterioration. Serious damage to plaster was evident in areas beneath the bridge structures surrounding the station. (Jack Muslovski photo, Cleveland Landmarks Press Collection)

Chicago, New York City, and Boston. When Amtrak announced the return of the passenger train to Cleveland, it decided that it would not operate out of CUT. Citing the crippling costs entailed by maintaining the giant facility for one arrival and one departure each day, Amtrak explained that it would be considerably less expensive to build a small new passenger station on the lakefront. Ironically, that station stands today just a few hundred feet from where the Group Plan union station would have been located.

With the end of Penn Central service, the only train still entering and leaving the cavernous station was the Erie-Lackawanna commuter. It continued for another few years, but finally it too met its end. Its last run from the Terminal came on January 14, 1977. That date marked the end of the Cleveland Union Terminal railroad era. It had lasted just short of 47 years.

In similar fashion, the early dreams of CUT as a hub for rapid transit failed to materialize as planned. When the Cleveland Interurban Railroad (renamed the Shaker Heights Rapid Transit after 1944 when its operation was taken over by the City of Shaker Heights) entered CUT in 1930, there were still three interurban lines serving the city, but their days were numbered, and their owners were in no position to reroute them into the new facility. The Cleveland Southwestern folded on January 29, 1931; the Northern Ohio on April 1, 1932; and the Lake Shore Electric on May 15, 1938.

For 25 years, the Shaker Heights Rapid Transit was without a transit partner at CUT. That changed on March 15, 1955, when the Cleveland Transit System (CTS) began operations on its new east side rapid transit line between Windermere and CUT. The line followed a right-of-way to East Cleveland which had been planned and partially built years earlier by the Van Sweringen brothers. The CTS Rapid was assigned station tracks 8-10, and instead of situating its downtown station in one of CUT's traction concourses, CTS chose instead to carve a new passenger entrance in the center of the former Ticket Lobby.

To better accommodate the anticipated increase in rapid transit patrons when the west side rapid transit began service to West 117th Street on August 14, another entrance was created in the West Traction Concourse, the first time that largely empty concourse experienced any real change. Subsequently the west side rapid line was extended twice, first to West Park in 1958, and then again in 1968 to Cleveland Hopkins International Airport. This last extension gave Cleveland the distinction of being the first U. S. city to have a direct rail link between its airport and downtown area. Although the CTS rapid began with great fanfare, the line never achieved the ridership that had been projected, and its West Concourse entrance was little used.

As railroad use of the terminal declined, the coach yard south of the station became superfluous. As another cost-conscious move, in 1970 Penn Central decided to convert the yard into a parking lot. In a way, the change seemed appropriate. It had been Americans' love for their

automobiles which had eroded the railroad passenger business. Stairways that once conveyed passengers to and from the train platforms below were put into service getting drivers to and from their cars.

While the coach yard conversion conveyed a certain irony, what happened next to the Steam Concourse could only be viewed as degrading. In 1971, its bronze chandeliers were replaced by flourescent fixtures, and below them, inside a chain link fence, two tennis courts were built. The times were clearly changing, but progress, this was not.

In 1975 Harvey's closed its English Oak Room restaurant. For 45 years it had been one of Cleveland's finest and most popular dining rooms. The absence of railroad traffic, the drop in rapid transit ridership (it had fallen by 33% since 1955), and a general decline in downtown Cleveland as the region's primary shopping area meant ever fewer evening diners. The restaurant could not survive on the lunch trade alone.

Reopening the skylight and putting furniture in the otherwise empty Main Concourse gave patrons of the food court in the adjacent East Traction Concourse a place to have a quick lunch. (Forest City Enterprises)

Plans for Tower City Center underwent many changes from the time of the first conceptual model in 1972. This sketch, which includes Phase 3 of the project, dates from the mid-1980s. (Forest City Enterprises)

The station's dark days were paralleled by the sagging fortunes of its owner. Penn Central Railroad declared bankruptcy in 1970, and trustees managed the company until 1975 when Conrail was established and took over Penn Central's transportation assets. A bankrupt owner of a facility which no longer served its needs meant that little would be spent to maintain, much less to upgrade the property. CUT's downslide accelerated.

CUT presented a depressing scene. Paint was peeling from the ceilings. In places chunks of plaster had broken free due to water seepage from the deteriorating bridge structures supporting the streets above. Security was lax, and gates had to be installed to prevent loiterers and vagrants from overrunning the complex.

The end of 1977 also marked the end of Fred Harvey's CUT lease. The company saw no signs that the fortunes of the station would rebound, and so the curtain came down on 47 years of Harvey's services in the Cleveland area.

At about the same time, the Ostendorf Morris Company of Cleveland was hired to see if it could inject some new life into the station. Approximately 600 rapid transit trains entered or departed the station each day, and an estimated 45,000 persons walked through the Terminal concourses each weekday on their way to work. If the station had something to offer, this substantial population could perhaps become more than passers by.

Slowly but steadily, improvements were made to the property. Security and maintenance were beefed up, and the ramps between the concourse level and Public Square were given a facelift. The tennis courts were removed, and the Steam Concourse was given a cleaning. A sheen returned to the marble walls as years of accumulated grime and stains were removed. Ostendorf Morris was able to secure new tenants to occupy some of the space formerly used by the Harvey operation, and a modest food court took shape in the East Traction Concourse.

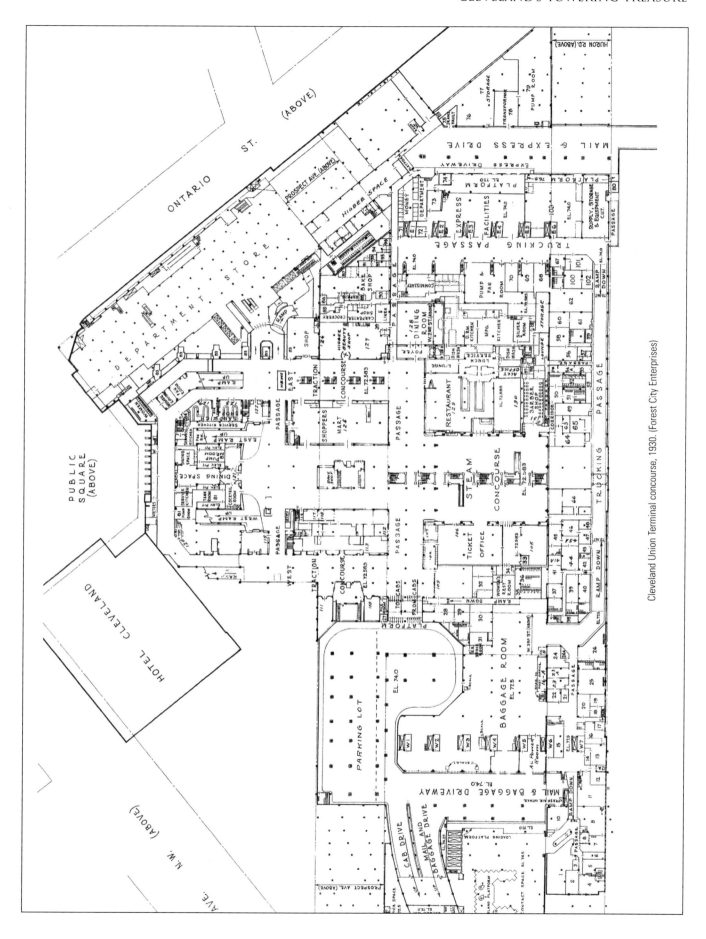

Cleveland Union Terminal concourse, 1930. (Forest City Enterprises)

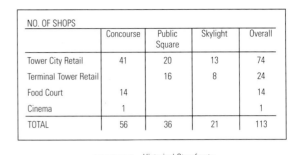

NO. OF SHOPS				
	Concourse	Public Square	Skylight	Overall
Tower City Retail	41	20	13	74
Terminal Tower Retail		16	8	24
Food Court	14			14
Cinema	1			1
TOTAL	56	36	21	113

‐ ‐ ‐ ‐   Historical Storefronts

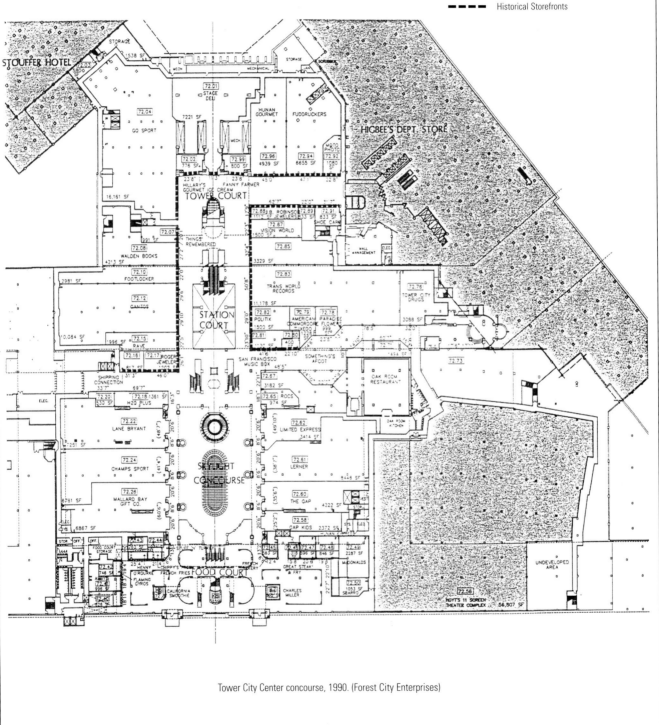

Tower City Center concourse, 1990. (Forest City Enterprises)

Tables and chairs were installed in the Main and East Traction concourse areas to encourage passers by to stop for a beverage or a snack.

In 1972, Sheldon Guren of Cleveland-based U. S. Realty Investments (USRI), the firm which then owned the Terminal Tower, had announced an ambitious plan for the total transformation of the station area. The Tower City plan, as it was named, would transform the concourse areas into a shopping mall and fill the acreage to the south of Huron Road down to the Cuyahoga River with new buildings. The plan envisioned a 1,000-room hotel, three office towers, a parking garage for 5,500 cars, a sports arena, an air cargo terminal, and several apartment buildings. The Tower City blueprint was created by the Cleveland firm of Dalton, Dalton, Little & Newport, and it carried a cost estimate of $250-300 million. Five years after it was first unveiled, the plan remained just that.

Then, in 1980 U. S. Realty Investments teamed up with Forest City Enterprises, another Cleveland firm, to form Tower City Properties. Forest City Enterprises was founded as a lumber company in 1921 by Charles Ratner. Soon joined by his brothers Leonard and Max, the company grew into a prime developer of suburban land. The Ratner family remained in charge as the company's reach and influence grew over the years. Leonard's son Albert became chief executive officer in 1975. Albert Ratner, his sister Ruth, and her first husband, Sam Miller, were the principals in redirecting Forest City's attention to downtown Cleveland. USRI's Guren, a long-time friend of the Ratners, had invited

Glitter lights all along the former Ticket Lobby helped make create a more friendly atmosphere for shoppers and commuters. (Forest City Enterprises)

Forest City to become half-owner of the Tower in 1974, and the business partners decided to move forward with the Tower City plans.

In 1980 the joint venture of U. S. Realty Investments and Forest City Enterprises bought the station area from the Cleveland Union Terminals Company for $8.5 million, and promised to inject new life into the facility. That year CUT marked its 50th anniversary, and observers hoped that the significant public interest generated by the anniversary celebration and the new ownership with its deep Cleveland roots would create the synergy to bring the Tower City project to life.

This map indicates the network of bridges that weave through the Tower City Center property lines. (Forest City Enterprises)

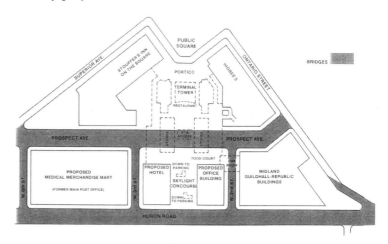

Bridge repairs were underway in 1984. This view shows work being done on the Huron Road structure. (Forest City Enterprises)

A major part of creating The Avenue was to add an additional floor of stores at the Public Square level of the complex. (Cleveland Landmarks Press Collection)

Soon signs of the new owners' energy became visible. One welcome development was the renovation of the Steam Concourse skylight, which had been sealed shut since the World War II years. Glass replaced the metal panels in the skylight's superstructure, and the tiles that covered the skylight itself were removed.

Natural light once again began to illuminate the interior. This was the first step in a plan to convert the concourse area into an indoor park, with plentiful greenery and seating, and to rehabilitate the adjoining spaces for retail and restaurant uses.

Other improvements soon followed. Glitter lights were installed along the arches of the Ticket Lobby area, the kiosks that had cluttered the central spaces of the Ticket Lobby were removed, and the brass store fronts in the East Traction and Ticket Lobby areas were cleaned. Leases were signed with new merchants, and by the 1981 Christmas shopping season, new businesses were lining the Ticket Lobby and the East Traction Concourse.

The eastern and southern sides of the East Traction Concourse hosted a variety of fast food outlets, and the concourse areas were furnished with tables and chairs. A variety of merchants signed leases for spaces in the Ticket Lobby. The West Traction Concourse, though, remained largely undeveloped, and so Tower City Properties decided to locate its offices there. Sand's Brass Door Restaurant moved into rehabilitated space at the lobby's northern end, in space that had formerly housed Harvey's Meeting Place and later the Choo-Choo Restaurant. A 45-foot Christmas tree, reminiscent of the trees that had once been a major Cleveland tradition at the old Sterling Lindner store, was set up in the Steam Concourse.

Although all these improvements were welcome and did restore some vitality to the station area, the larger Tower City development remained a vision for the future. Cleveland's corps of perpetual skeptics muttered that the Tower City

60

concept was just another one of those "phantom" projects: announcements in the media to test the waters for potential interest but something that would never materialize. Two more substantial reasons, however, bore the main responsibility for the ensuing delays.

The chief reason for the plan's failure to move forward was an unresolved dispute over who was responsible for repairing the bridge structures which carried Huron Road, Prospect Avenue, and West Second, Third, and Sixth streets over the station property. Over the years, the bridges in the project area had shown signs of considerable deterioration, and periodic repairs had been of temporary rather than permanent nature. The bridges actually consisted of 36 self-standing sections, and every one of the expansion joints between the sections had become defective, allowing salt to eat into the concrete and structural steel below. As a result, water from above leaked into the station, damaging the ceilings in the traction lobbies and the English Oak Room. Plaster damage was extensive. Until the bridge problem was solved, it would have been pointless to move forward with the Tower City plans.

The Ordinance of 1919 specified that the City of Cleveland would be the agent responsible for the upkeep of the surfaces, curbs, sidewalks, and water lines supported by the bridgework in the CUT area. The ordinance further stipulated that the Cleveland Union Terminals Company would have responsibility for maintaining the underlying structural steel bridge work.

Because of the mutual responsibilities involved with the Terminal bridges, each party wanted the majority of the blame

Restoring the water-damaged English Oak Room to its original splendor was a painstaking task. This view shows the work in progress. (Forest City Enterprises)

(and the cost of repairs) to be borne by the other. In the 1970s, during the Perk and Kucinich mayoral administrations, the city was facing serious financial problems and was in no position to assume the costs entailed in repairing the bridge structures. Nor was the bankrupt station owner. Tower City's failure to get underway was due, at least in part, to the inability of the parties to settle the bridge repair problem.

The second cause for the delay in implementing the Tower City plan was the 1981 decision reached by U. S. Realty Investments to liquidate its real estate portfolio. That decision, of course, impacted

the capacity of the Tower City Properties management team to move forward with its plans. In October 1982 Forest City Enterprises became sole owner of the station property when it paid $5.5 million for the half interest that had belonged to USRI.

While the ownership issue was being resolved, there was also progress being made on the bridge repairs. George Voinovich, who became Cleveland mayor in 1980, recognized that if the city was to get out of the doldrums that beset it, the most likely approach would be through public-private partnerships. Voinovich also had a financing tool at his disposal, the federal government's Urban Development Action Grant (UDAG) program. Recognizing the importance of the Tower City proposal, he tapped into that funding source to support rebuilding the five Terminal area bridges. Additional financing came from the Urban Mass

Transit Authority (UMTA) and the Ohio Department of Transportation (ODOT).

The Cleveland firm of Kiewit Eastern Co. was successful bidder for the bridge work. Work on rebuilding the nearly 3,200 feet of bridge structure began on February 29, 1984. The concrete surfaces were removed to get at the structural element. Worn structural steel was replaced, and a new drainage system was installed. Then a new deck, requiring 350 tons of steel and 38,000 square yards of concrete, was put in place. The total project cost $18 million. It was completed in October 1986, much to the relief of downtown drivers.

The bridge repairs meant that the major hurdle to the project had been overcome, but another obstacle remained in the way. To make the Tower City concept attractive to the public, it was necessary to provide adequate parking space. One solution to free up sufficient parking space involved consolidating the track arrangement for the terminal's two rapid transit lines into one station area. The Greater Cleveland Regional Transit Authority (RTA) was willing to undertake the project, but funding had to be secured. That arrived in the form of another UDAG grant, with additional support from the Urban Mass Transit Administration. The relocation of the Shaker lines (Blue and Green lines) to the central station area which served the Airport-Windermere (Red) line and designing and building a new station to serve both lines was budgeted at $44 million. The station project was tied into a need to revise track access to the Terminal and to improve the right-of-way from East 37th Street to Fulton Road. The added costs for the track

and signal work increased the entire project budget to $60 million.

With most of the hurdles then out of the way, Forest City Enterprises selected RTKL Architects, a Dallas architectural firm, to provide overall design for the Tower City Center renovations. Associate architect was Cleveland-based Teare, Herman & Gibans. The architects had been instructed as much as possible to preserve the old station's distinctive features. That goal was intended to make the project eligible for historic preservation tax credits. That target, however, was not achieved. The National Parks Service, which administers the historic credits program, objected to several features of the renovation. These included the elimination of the Prospect

The new Skylight Concourse is well along. Grand opening of Tower City Center is just two months away, January 1990. (Forest City Enterprises)

Escalators take rapid transit riders to and from the new Regional Transit Authority station at track level. (Forest City Enterprises)

Arcade pedestrian passageway from Prospect Avenue to the Terminal Tower Portico, construction of an additional shopping floor between the concourse and the Public Square levels, and replacement of the old Steam Concourse Skylight with a larger and higher one. Creating sufficient space to make the renovation economically feasible, however, made those changes necessary, and so Forest City Enterprises chose to proceed without the tax credits.

After several years of planning and design, a formal groundbreaking for Tower City Center took place on November 6, 1986. Work on the project, however, could not actually begin until July 1988, when the leases of the station-area tenants expired. Shortly thereafter, wooden barricades were erected to separate the construction zone from the passageways needed by people who parked in

the track level lot and those embarking or disembarking the rapid transit lines. While the barricades were necessary for pedestrian safety, they rendered the remarkable changes underway largely invisible to the thousands who had to thread their way through the narrow passages they formed.

One part of the renovation, though not very glamorous, was critical to its success. Additional parking was needed. To meet this need, engineers found that they could squeeze in a second deck of parking between the former track level and the concourse level in the area where the railroad passenger platforms had been located. Elevator and escalator lobbies connected the parking levels to the retail areas above. More parking was developed in the area vacated by the Shaker Rapid lines' former storage tracks and from space opened up by the move of the Post Office from its old home to its new headquarters on Orange Avenue. Enlarging the parking areas resulted in space for 2,340 cars.

The concourse area, of course, was the main focus of the renovation project, and dramatic changes there transformed the former station spaces into a spectacular shopping mall, named The Avenue at Tower City Center. The former traction concourses disappeared to create a larger floor print for the shops that would line the central concourse area. To this central space a second floor of retail space was added at the Public Square level. This new level was accessed directly from the Portico and stretched south to Huron Road. Creation of this new level left behind an interesting detail, an indicator of the earlier arrangement. The two passages which lead from the Portico to the new shopping level are now level, but the angled ceiling above is a reminder that they were once ramps leading down to the Ticket Lobby.

The concourse interior is divided into three court areas, the Tower Court, the Station Court, and the Skylight Court.

The Tower Court is at the northern end of the mall space. It was carved from the area formerly occupied by the Prospect Arcade. Its central space, dominated by a domed skylight, is surrounded by three levels of balconies and served by a bank of escalators. Beneath the skylight, at the Concourse Level, is a waterfall fountain, into which visitors annually toss thousands of dollars of coins (which Forest City Enterprises distributes to local charities). Its marble floor is a survivor from the station era. The new Public Square Level is occupied by shops. The Prospect Level is

home to the Greater Cleveland Partnership (which also occupies a part of the top level) and connects to a passageway to the Higbee Building.

The middle space of The Avenue is known as the Station Court, so named because it is where the RTA rapid transit station is located (and where formerly the CTS station had been built in 1955). The new station was designed by the Cannon Partnership of Grand Island, New York, with Whitley/Whitley of Shaker Heights as the associate architect.

The station is located at the facility's lowest (track) level. It can be reached from the Concourse, Public Square or Prospect levels by stairways, escalators, or elevator. At the center of the station is a lobby with fare box entrances leading to the Blue and Green line platforms at its eastern end and to the Red line platforms at its western end.

The tasteful Ritz-Carlton Hotel lobby gives guests their first sense of just how comfortable their stay in the new hotel will be. (Forest City Enterprises)

Separate boarding areas were deemed a practical solution to the challenge caused by RTA using high-platform loading trains on its Red line but low-platform loading cars on its Blue and Green lines. Each boarding area is penetrated by three tracks, one a stub track ending in the loading area, and the other two as through tracks. One additional track, in the former Shaker Heights Rapid Transit area, was retained as an emergency through track.

The most dramatic and the largest portion of the Tower City concourse is the Skylight Court, which occupies the area where the Steam Concourse was once located. The Skylight Court extends south from the Prospect Avenue line to Huron Road. Its most striking feature is its barrel-arched skylight which rises 80 feet above the concourse level. Below the skylight is an elliptical pool which features pulsating fountain jets which are often synchronized to music. At the court's northern end a graceful curved stairway leads up to the Public Square level. The stairway also serves as a stage for the entertainment which is frequently presented in the court.

Two levels of balconies frame the Skylight Court, one at the Public Square level, and the higher one at the Huron Road level. At the southern end of the court, in a space opened up by the removal of the wall that once held the Ferro mural, is a two-level fast-food court and an escalator bank which leads to the parking levels below.

Through the skylight two new towers can be seen, one to each side. In Van Sweringen days, this location had been intended for another office building, but after setting the foundation designed with the strength to support a 25-story tower, the project was stalled by the onset of the Depression. Tower City engineers found that the foundation was solid and could still serve as the base for new construction. This significantly reduced the cost for developing the new towers, and eased the decision to proceed with the new buildings.

The eastern site became home to the 12-story Skylight Office Tower, which has 338,000 square feet of leaseable space. It has entrances from both The Avenue and from West Second Street. The western site was developed as a combination hotel and office tower, the Ritz Carlton/Chase Financial Tower. The office building and the hotel share the first floor level, which adjoins the Huron Road level of The

Avenue. They can also be reached from West Third Street. The office component of the structure has 130,000 square feet of leaseable space on floors two through five.

Elevators whisk Ritz-Carlton Hotel guests from the first floor entrance lobby to the formal guest lobby on the sixth floor. A total of 208 luxurious guest rooms are situated on floors seven through 14. These include 28 suites and 47 club rooms. The seventh floor also houses a fitness center, saunas, and a swimming pool. The hotel also has a Grand Ballroom as well as eight smaller meeting rooms. The Ritz-Carlton's popular Century dining room is situated off the entry lobby and can also be reached from The Avenue's Skylight Court.

By March 1990 The Avenue shopping mall was nearing completion, and the hotel and office buildings were not too far behind. The Avenue retail area covered some 450,000 square feet, of which 361,000 represented leasable space, designed to accommodate 110 stores. It also contained an 11-screen movie theater, which returned first-run features to the downtown audience for the first time in a decade. The entire project cost just under $388 million (about $549 million in 2004 prices).

Grand opening ceremonies were set for March 29, 1990, and on that day a lavish celebration marked the event. Thousands of Clevelanders made their way downtown to take in the ceremonies and to explore the glittering facility and its exciting array of distinguished shops, many new to the Cleveland area. While no one took an actual count, reporters estimated that nearly two million Greater Clevelanders strolled the Avenue in its first month of operation. What had long been a key

component of Cleveland's best known address had been given a new lease on life, and it injected new vitality to the city center. That was indeed an accomplishment that the local population deemed worthy to celebrate.

Not everything that Tower City planners had envisioned took place. Phase Three of the project called for extending the center by new construction south of Huron Road and stretching down to the river. These plans included a new department store, more office buildings, and apartments and condominiums. For a while it appeared that the city's new Rock and Roll Hall of Fame and Museum would be located on the site, but that plan fizzled, and the facility was instead built on the lakefront.

The Carl B. Stokes Federal Courthouse, located at the western end of the former railroad coach yard, as seen from the Terminal Tower, was completed in 2002. (J. A. Toman photo)

In 2003 a blue ribbon committee chose the site for a new convention center. If that plan had moved forward, Forest City Enterprises pledged to develop not only the convention facility, but to implement its long dormant proposal for a residential community on the land it owns on the Scranton Peninsula just across the river. A pedestrian bridge would have connected the Peninsula with Tower City Center. Hopes for the exciting development were dashed when pollsters found that

Cuyahoga County voters were not disposed to approve a tax hike to fund the convention center. Rather than face a defeat at the ballot, the political leadership withdrew its support for the issue.

Some additional Tower City Center construction, however, has taken place. In 1994 the Regional Transit Authority built an interior Walkway to Gateway. It stretches from the southeastern end of the Tower City food court to connect with the new sports facilities at Gateway. The walkway connects directly with the lobby of Gund Arena. Jacobs Field is just a short walk beyond. The passageway made taking the rapid transit to basketball and baseball games more appealing, and it made the Skylight Court a popular location to rendezvous with friends before game time.

In 2002 the Tower City Amphitheater made its debut. The outdoor concert pavilion, housed in a tent-like structure south of Canal Road and connected to the Avenue by shuttle bus service, can accommodate crowds of about 4,000. The amphitheater was intended both as an outdoor stage for summer concerts and as a venue for popular downtown events such as the annual rib cook-off.

In 2003 another walkway from the food court area opened to the west, connecting Tower City Center to the new Carl B. Stokes Federal Courthouse at the corner of Huron Road and West Ninth Street. The site is on the western edge of what had been part of the center's surface parking area and of the earlier railroad coach yard.

The courthouse, first announced for the city in 1994, took eight years to bring to completion. The process for selecting the location for the new facility took two years before the Tower City site won out (it was then purchased by the federal government for $18.3 million). The courthouse was designed by the Boston firm of Kallmann, McKinnell and Wood (KMW) under the auspices of the General Services Administration. Excavation on the site began in 1998, and construction continued until August 2002.

The gleaming white 24-story court tower rises 430-feet and provides 700,000 square feet of space. The building has an unusual profile. Its curved western facade gives the building a massive look. The angled eastern side is not quite so imposing but still conveys mass, but from the north and south, the building is at its narrowest point and looks almost fragile. Total cost for the courthouse was $192 million.

Whether the judges who preside over the court tower's 16 courtrooms make use of the walkway to have lunch in the fast food court is not known, but undoubtedly some of the other federal workers do, as do some of the hundreds of persons who daily have business to conduct with the federal court. The courthouse clearly is a net plus for the shops on The Avenue.

The Tower City Center project injected a vibrant new life into the faded fortunes of the Cleveland Union Terminal. Once again the former concourse area is filled by milling crowds. And as in years past, when Greater Clevelanders decide where to meet downtown, chances are that they will choose The Avenue of Tower City Center just as they once chose the old Steam Concourse.

Just as Cleveland Union Terminal opened during the Great Depression, so

Tower City Center opened as Cleveland's downtown economy was facing a downturn. The development of new upscale suburban shopping centers, the loss of downtown's two remaining department stores, and the growth of suburban office parks in Beachwood, Independence, and North Olmsted posed real challenges for Tower City management. These in turn have hindered the plans to proceed with Phase Three of Tower City Center.

The future, of course, cannot be foretold. But odds are that when the time is opportune, the advantages of the distinguished Tower City Center setting will once again set in motion a renewed period of growth. As the remake of the old Union Terminal so clearly has demonstrated, good ideas have resilience. The proven track record of Forest City Enterprises and its compelling vision for the future adds further assurance that the future will only add more luster to the grand complex at the very heart of the city.

Clevelanders have quickly grown fond of a new downtown Christmas holiday tradition: the airships patrolling the Skylight Concourse. (Forest City Enterprises)

The Tower

OBSERVATION SODA GRILL
43RD FLOOR, TERMINAL TOWER, CLEVELAND

The entire Terminal project began with the Van Sweringens' interest in building a Public Square station for their Shaker Heights rapid transit line. The plan then evolved into a joint interurban-passenger railroad station. The office tower that was built above the station was, as Tower historian Walter Leedy terms it, an "afterthought" (cf. Leedy in reference list). Yet it has been that afterthought which for 75 years has been Cleveland's most famous landmark and which continues its preeminence in the collective consciousness of Clevelanders. While the Terminal Tower has been surpassed in height by the Key Tower, and almost overwhelmed by the mass of the BP Tower, it has not ceded its primacy of place as the city's foremost symbol.

As for the station, architect for the Tower was the Chicago firm of Graham, Anderson, Probst & White. Besides their work on the Terminal group, there are only two other examples of their work in the city. One is the 1931 upper-floors addition to the May Company Building. The other is the 21-story Huntington Building

(originally the Union Trust and later the Union Commerce Building) at East Ninth Street and Euclid Avenue, which opened in 1924.

Students of architecture see in the neoclassical Terminal Tower design similarities with the New York City Municipal Building (1911), designed by one of the firm's predecessors, McKim, Meade and White of New York City. There is also a resemblance to the Wrigley Building in Chicago, a 1921 Graham, Anderson, Probst & White design, but the Terminal Complex in Cleveland represents the firm's most famous achievement.

Although work on site clearing and excavation had begun some three years earlier, the official groundbreaking for

The Huntington Building at East Ninth Street and Euclid Avenue was designed by Graham, Anderson, Probst & White. The columned first-floor entranceway bears some resemblance to their later work on the Terminal Tower. (J. A. Toman photo)

One of the earliest Graham, Anderson, Probst & White designs for the Terminal office building lacked the towering center piece that would make it a lasting Cleveland landmark. (Cleveland Picture Collection of Cleveland Public Library)

The architectural rendering of the Terminal Tower. While the Tower was substantially drawn as it would look, the yet to be finalized Higbee Building (at the left) would still undergo significant changes. (Cleveland Union Terminal Archives of the Cleveland State University Libraries)

Cleveland's most famous landmark, the Terminal Tower, took place on September 28, 1923. General contractor for the project was the Cleveland firm of John Gill and Sons. The Van Sweringens' Cleveland Terminals Building Company was in charge of the project.

When the Public Square project was first announced, the accompanying sketch for the office building which would rise above the station showed a relatively squat structure. The 1918 drawing shows a building rising some 14 stories and then crowned with a cupola style central core of about five additional floors. Before construction actually began, however, the plan underwent a momentous change. The Vans recognized how attractive office space in the new location would be, and more space meant more lease revenue. As a result, the cupola was replaced by a central tower that would rise another 38 floors above the 14-story base.

Some newspaper accounts at the time attributed the change to the Van

Sweringens' concern that the cupola design resembled too closely a German army helmet and that in sensitivity to unhappy memories people still had of World War I, they ordered the change. It is not likely that the Vans were that politically sensitive.

The Terminal Tower formed the most dramatic feature of a construction concept known as "air rights." Air rights involve erecting one building above the property of another, in this case the Tower over the Station. At the time, the Terminal Group represented one of the most extensive uses of that concept, one later used in planning and construction of New York's Rockefeller Center. In a way it can be said that the Terminal Tower has no basement. The Station's concourse level is where a basement might have been found.

Although the Terminal Tower does not have a basement, it rests on a very firm foundation. In Cleveland, foundations for tall building pose a challenge. Unlike New York City (the skyscraper capital of the world, where bedrock is fairly near the surface), Cleveland, on the shores of Lake Erie, has a great deal of clay resting above its bedrock level. Thus excavation and foundation work for tall buildings in Cleveland is both complex and costly. The Terminal Tower's foundation was laid by the caisson method. The entire terminal project required 55 caissons, 17 of which anchored the Tower building. Pits for the Tower were dug down 250 feet to reach bedrock. To reach that point, the excavators had to burrow through several layers of clay of varying consistency. In some places it was hard and dry. In others it was damp and viscous. Somehow the legend developed

that the Terminal Tower was built on quicksand. That was not the case. It was probably the putty-like nature of some levels of clay that gave rise to the "quicksand" embellishment.

Work on the foundation also gave rise to another myth, that two men are buried beneath the Tower. In October 1928 two construction workers were laboring in a pit which had been dug for the concrete foundations of the Prospect Avenue bridge structure. Patrick Cleary and Patrick Toolis were at the bottom of the pit, 103 feet deep, when the dirt wall of the pit in which they were working gave way from the weight of concrete newly poured into an adjacent

Caissons such as this one gave the Terminal Complex a foundation reaching down to bedrock. (Cleveland Union Terminal Archives of the Cleveland State University Libraries)

shaft. The men had no chance at all. Fifty tons of fast-hardening concrete engulfed them. It took rescue workers 18 hours to dig through the congealing mess in order to recover their bodies. No one is buried beneath the complex.

With the foundation in place, the first piece of structural steel was bolted into place on October 18, 1926. Steel erection

THE TERMINAL TOWER BUILDIN
CLEVELAND, OHIO
H. D. JOUETT, Chief Engineer
GRAHAM, ANDERSON, PROBST & WHITE, Archit
JOHN GILL & SONS, Contractors

The 14-story base of the Terminal Tower is substantially complete in this February 1927 construction photo. (Cleveland Union Terminal Archives of the Cleveland State University Libraries)

the cost of materials and labor for putting up the Tower amounted to some $11,000,000. At today's rates, to duplicate the feat would cost over $110 million.

The Terminal Tower fronts onto the southwest quadrant of Public Square. From its northern exposure, it can basically be described as consisting of a central shaft that rises 52 stories above the ground, with two 14-story arms angling away from the center and embracing the outer perimeter of the Square. On the southern side of the Tower, two additional wings, also 14 stories tall, extend from the central shaft to the Prospect Avenue line.

It is the central core that really forms the popular visual image of the Tower. It rises evenly through the 28th floor, where the first structural change takes place. There the outer facing changes from limestone to terra cotta. The central core continues from the 29th through the 34th floor levels with the same dimensions, 98 feet square, but four pillars, extending from the 31st to the 33rd floor, break the smooth lines that mark the lower stories.

After the 34th floor the Tower narrows, but retains it basic square shape. Starting at the 37th floor, the Tower takes on a cylindrical shape. Additional pillars grace the 41st through the 43rd floor levels. At the 44th floor, the building narrows once again, and as it moves towards its 52nd-story peak, its shape become conical.

The Terminal Tower easily outpaced the Ohio Bell Building (now SBC Building) on Huron Road for the title of the city's tallest. Designed by the Cleveland partnership of Hubbell & Benes, the Ohio Bell Building was completed just months before the final steel was put into place for

proceeded rapidly, with the last piece of steel being hoisted into place at the 52nd floor level on August 18, 1927.

The cornerstone was laid on March 16, 1927. The task of attaching the limestone outer skin to the steel skeleton proceeded right along with the steel work, though at a slower pace.

Enormous amounts of material were consumed in building the Tower. The tower required over 55,000 barrels of cement; 17,800 tons of steel; 118,230 tons of granite, limestone, and terra cotta; 2,200 windows; some ten miles of water pipe; and some 71 miles of wiring. At the time, the Terminal Tower. The telephone company's new home reached 360 feet. Officially the Terminal Tower is listed as rising 708 feet, a measurement taken from the concourse level of the Union Station. It rises 786 feet above Lake Erie, and its apex stands 916 feet above the bedrock foundation. Rising above the Tower is a 65-foot flag pole, so that to the very tip of the pole, the height reached is 773 feet. Flag poles, however, are not counted as being part of the basic structure of a building; hence the 708 feet to the base of

the pole constitutes the Terminal Tower's officially accepted height.

When the Terminal Tower reached its 708-foot mark, it became the second tallest building in the United States. The only building taller was the Woolworth Building (1913) in New York City. It climbed to 792 feet. Over the next six years, though, six more buildings in New York passed the Terminal Tower in height, the two best known being the Chrysler Building (1930) at 1,046 feet, and the Empire State Building (1931) at 1,250 feet.

As the structural steel is hoisted into place for the Tower's upper floors, the limestone facade is being applied to the lower stories, June 1927. (Cleveland Union Terminal Archives of the Cleveland State University Libraries)

By August 1927, the structural steel work on the Tower is nearing completion. (Cleveland Union Terminal Archives of the Cleveland State University Libraries)

These 1930 New York buildings made the Terminal Tower the nation's eighth tallest building, a position it held for 34 years. It had the added distinction of being the tallest building in the United States outside New York City. It maintained that privileged slot until 1964 when it was surpassed by the 750-foot Prudential Center in Boston.

Demand for office space in subsequent years prompted a proliferation of tall towers throughout the country. As a result, in 2004 Cleveland's venerable Terminal Tower is ranked as only the 93rd tallest building in the United States. Seventeen cities besides New York have at least one building taller than the Terminal. The tallest building in the country at the present time is Chicago's Sears Tower (1974) which rises 1,454 feet and numbers 110 stories.

After the Tower was completed, Cleveland did not see construction of

Facade work on the Terminal
Tower continues. The areas not
being fitted with a limestone
exterior will eventually be connected to the Higbee Building,
not yet underway, October 1927.
(Herbert H. Harwood Collection)

The upper floors of the Tower show both its changing shape and its ornamental detail. (Cleveland *Press* Collection of the Cleveland State University Libraries)

The Terminal Tower is complete. In the right background, between the Tower and the Republic Building can be seen the Ohio Bell (now SBC) Building on Huron Road. (Herbert H. Harwood Collection)

another tall office building for another quarter century. That drought finally ended when the Illuminating Building, across Public Square from the Terminal Tower, opened in 1957. At 22 stories and 300 feet, it was no rival to the Terminal Tower. In 1964, the 40-story Tower at Erieview, the centerpiece of the Erieview urban renewal area along East Ninth Street, made its appearance. It rose to 529 feet.

The first real Cleveland rival for the Terminal Tower was the Sohio Building (now the BP Tower). In July 1977 the firm of Cushman-Wakefield of New York City had proposed a $70 million headquarters building for the Standard Oil Company of Ohio on the location of the old coach yards. The plan would have provided for a 22-story office building, with an atrium connecting the office tower to a completely redesigned Union Terminal Steam Concourse. All told, the plan would have provided 975,000 square feet of space. The City of Cleveland was to have contributed towards the repair of the bridges as its share of the project. Once again the bridge issue proved a snag, and time for the project expired. It was declared dead in July 1978.

Then in 1982 Sohio announced a new plan for a headquarters building at the southeast quadrant of Public Square. The new skyscraper would rise 45 stories and reach 658 feet, just 50 feet shorter than the Terminal Tower. At the time, commentators believed this limiting decision was made as a sign of respect for the city's landmark building. At the urging of the Cleveland City Planning Commission, the Sohio architects, Hellmuth, Obata & Kassabaum of St. Louis, had also agreed to trim the building's upper-story profile with four setbacks so that it reflected the narrowing profile of the Terminal Tower's top stories.

Such deference, if that is what it really was, came to an end when the Cleveland Planning Commission voted in 1987 to authorize a 900-foot ceiling for the new Society Center project on the northeast quadrant of Public Square. On October 30, 1990, the structural steel work on the Society Tower (now Key Tower) passed the 708-foot mark, and the Terminal Tower became Cleveland's second tallest building. When Society Tower was completed in 1991, it stood at 888 feet, with 57 floors of office space. Its 60-foot spire raises its total height to 948 feet, 175 feet above the tip of the Terminal Tower flag pole.

Time has thus eclipsed the distinction the Terminal Tower 's height once enjoyed, but to a remarkable degree it has retained its soaring image. With its slender profile, the setbacks, and the change of shape marking its upper stories, the Terminal Tower seems taller than it actually is. With an eye to cost, contemporary developers typically sponsor towers that are fundamentally boxlike in design. Such restraints did not limit the Terminal Tower's more grandiose conception. Nor was the imposing plan limited only to the upper stories. Its impressive character began right at ground level.

The main entranceway to the Tower fronts on Public Square. It features seven large arches, interspersed by six Ionic-styled columns. Each arch measures 18 feet across and 35 feet high. They frame a set of bronze doorways, surmounted by mullioned glass rising to the apex of the archway and flooding the interior portico

with natural light. Since its earliest days, the entrance has served as the backdrop for myriad public events. It forms a scene immediately recognizable to Greater Clevelanders.

Through the entranceway lies the Portico, a 153-foot long grand hall. To both ends of the Portico, mirrored panels rise above portals that lead to what had formerly been the traction lobbies. The traction lobbies also connect the Tower to its

The first Cleveland Building to rival the Terminal Tower was the Sohio Building (now the BP Tower). The Terminal's Observation Deck provided a great spot to watch the new building grow, May 1984. (J. A. Toman photo)

adjoining buildings, the Renaissance Cleveland Hotel to the west and the former Higbee/Dillard department store to the east. Off the eastern entryway was an ornate banking lobby originally occupied by the Union Trust Company (and now home to Brooks Brothers). Just beyond it, a curving ramp led to the East Traction Concourse (the ramp was removed during the Tower City renovations). Another ramp from the west passageway reached down to the West Traction Concourse. It too was removed for the Tower City project.

Reached directly from the Portico is the Terminal Tower's own lobby and to either side of it passageways which formerly led to the Concourse Ticket Lobby. These now connect directly to The Avenue shopping mall. Before the Tower City renovations, a stairway from the elevator lobby led up to the Prospect Arcade which was lined with shops and provided access to the Prospect level Higbee's men's store. Removal of the Arcade permitted construction of the Tower Court. Replacing the stairway is a short passage that leads to The Avenue's Tower Court. In 2004 Forest City officials installed there a Tower City Center Hall of Fame, recognizing individuals who had played a key role in the center's development. The members of the Hall of Fame include Herbert Strawbridge of The Higbee Company; Howard Schulman and Sheldon Guren of U.S.R.I.; J. Maurice Struchen of Society Bank; and Ruth Ratner Miller of Forest City Enterprises.

The Portico is an impressive room, conveying a sense of spaciousness and elegance. Its floor is of Tennessee marble, its walls of Botticino marble. The northern wall consists largely of the five archway windows. The vaulted ceiling, 47 feet high, is made of precast ornamental plaster. Seven murals grace the upper portions of the portico, the work of New York artist Jules Guerin, who had also painted murals for Graham, Anderson, Probst & White's Union Trust Building. Set off by a cream-painted border, the murals depict commerce, industry, transportation, and the four elements: water, fire, air, and earth. Five bronze chandeliers hang from the ceiling. Technically, the Portico was not part of the Terminal Tower, but of the Union Station below. The Tower's property line began just through the portico.

The graceful arches that form the Public Square entranceway to Tower City Center often display signs of the season. Here they celebrate Independence Day. (J. A. Toman photo)

The Portico is the grand entry hall to the Terminal Complex. (Forest City Enterprises)

Off the Terminal Tower's lobby are two elevator lobbies with four banks of elevators, each programmed to serve different ranges of floors. Originally manually operated, the elevators, which travel at 800 feet per minute, were converted to automatic service in 1969. The high rise elevators only reach to the 32nd floor. There passengers move to another set of elevators which continue to the 42nd floor. Altogether, counting the freight lifts (still manually operated and located elsewhere in the building), there are 27 elevators. The upper floors can also be reached by staircase. Though, in general, reserved for emergency use, the stairs to the top have often intrigued Clevelanders. They became the focus of the 2002 Tackle the Tower charity event to benefit Ronald McDonald House. The staircase with its 899 steps to the 42nd floor observation floor posed an interesting challenge for the hearty and determined climbers.

There is no elevator service above the 42nd floor. A standard staircase leads from

From the Terminal Tower Lobby a stairway formerly led to the Prospect Arcade. This was removed during the Tower City Center renovations. (Forest City Enterprises)

Just off the Portico, this ornate banking room was built for the Union Trust Company, a close collaborator with the Van Sweringen brothers. It is now the home to the Brooks Brothers store. (Forest City Enterprises)

the 42nd to the 44th floor. Then, from the 44th floor to the 51st, the only means of ascent is via a narrow spiraling metal stairway that runs through the center of each level. The top floor, the 52nd, is reached only by means of a metal ladder.

At first, this arrangement may seem somewhat strange, but no public access above the 43rd floor was ever intended. For a short time, that floor housed a Harvey's soda fountain. The top nine floors are really too small ever to have served any practical commercial purpose. They were built solely for aesthetic purposes, giving the building its pyramidal top and additional height. The top floors were meant to convey the soaring prospects of the city and of the Van Sweringen empire.

Tenant space in the Tower reaches from the second through the 43rd floor. The last office floor is the 41st. For their own offices, the Van Sweringen brothers selected the 36th floor and commissioned there a luxurious suite paneled in oak from the Sherwood Forest. The 42nd floor has served intermittently as an observation deck and as a conference room. The 43rd floor, home to the short-lived soda fountain, more recently housed communications equipment.

Over the years, the 42nd floor observation deck was one of the chief attractions of the Tower. When the deck first opened on May 17, 1928, a long line of Clevelanders waited patiently in line for their turn to get a bird's-eye view of the city. The throngs of visitors continued uninterrupted for the next 49 years. Records indicate that annually 50,000-100,000 visitors took advantage of the high-rise opportunity.

The deck's guest book reveals that visitors came not just from the Greater Cleveland area, but from every state of the Union and from just about every country in the world.

Following their two-elevator ride to the deck, visitors were treated to a panoramic view of the city. On a clear day, from that height a person could see for a distance of 32 miles. Claims which some visitors registered, that they could see Canada from the deck, are not true; the Canadian shoreline is some 55 miles distant. Because of the curvature of the earth and the height of the 42nd floor, the 32- mile limit represents the maximum distance one can see.

The "Ashby Leach Incident" brought a temporary end to public access to the observation deck. On August 26, 1976, a disgruntled Leach, a former railroad employee, staged an armed siege of the Chesapeake & Ohio Railroad's 36th floor executive suite to protest the railroad's hiring practices, which he felt ignored the needs of Viet Nam veterans. Leach held 13 persons hostage at gunpoint, but after nine hours of negotiation, the confrontation ended without casualties. The incident nonetheless left C&O officials acutely aware of a lack of security. The easiest remedy was to limit public access to the upper floors. With that goal in mind, the railroad negotiated a lease for the 42nd floor for use as a conference room. Thus, in April 1977, the observation deck was closed to the public, and a security station was established on the 32nd floor to keep unauthorized visitors from the elevators that served the top ten floors occupied by the railroad.

Clevelanders lamented their lost access to the observation deck, and soon

the media mounted a campaign to reopen the attraction. A compromise solution was reached, and beginning on summer weekends in 1982, visitors could once again make the trek to the 42nd floor. In 1983 the observation deck was also opened on weekends during the Christmas shopping season. In 1984, the visiting season was extended once again. The Cleveland Convention and Visitors' Bureau assumed the responsibility for conducting the tours to the observation deck tour.

The observation deck was closed again following the tragic events of 9/11/01.

The pennant below the U. S. flag indicates that the Cleveland Indians are playing a home game. The traffic on West Third Street is on its way to Cleveland Stadium during the 1954 American League Pennant season. (Robert Runyon photo, Cleveland Landmarks Press Collection)

Since then, it has only been opened to the public once, that during the Tower City Center WinterFest in 2003.

The observation deck is one of Cleveland's best known attractions, but the Tower also houses one of the city's best kept secrets: the fabled but little-known Greenbrier Suite (named for the C&O's famous Greenbrier Resort after the railroad leased the rooms). While the Tower was under construction, the Van Sweringen brothers decided they needed a home away from home, so that on occasions when the press of business kept them downtown until late at night, they would not be required to make the time-consuming trek back to their Daisy Hill home in Hunting Valley.

They commissioned favorite architect Philip Small to design their hideaway. The result was truly elegant. Built into an area of the Tower that actually intrudes on the space of the adjoining hotel building on the Square, it occupies parts of the 12th,

OBSERVATION SODA GRILL
43RD FLOOR, TERMINAL TOWER, CLEVELAND

Scraping the sky—
a cheerful fountain offers you
the pause that refreshes

UP you go, over 700 feet above Lake Erie, almost to the top of Terminal Tower, center structure of Cleveland's magnificent new "city within a city." High above all, a sparkling fountain and comfortable chairs around tables invite you to pause and refresh yourself with ice-cold Coca-Cola. One glimpse through a window gives a review of a great city's tremendous accomplishments—a spectacle that has inspired visitors from all over the world. Calm and relaxed, you

realize how great the pause that refreshes often can be . . . Of course it is interesting. Yet it is so natural. The pause that refreshes has come to be so much a part of custom that no modern office building is complete without a fountain serving Coca-Cola. Terminal Tower also has its ground-floor fountain service. The popu-

larity of Coca-Cola, with that tingling, delicious taste and its cool after-sense of refreshment, has made it ready for you everywhere.

THE BEST SERVED DRINK IN THE WORLD
A pure drink of natural flavors served in its own thin, crystal-like glass. This glass insures the right proportions of Coca-Cola syrup and ice-cold carbonated water. The final touches are to add a little finely chipped ice and stir with a spoon until the sparkling bubbles bead at the brim. The Coca-Cola Company, Atlanta, Ga.

OVER **8** MILLION A DAY

It had to be good to get where it is

13th, and 14th floors. A private stairway from the suite reaches down to the seventh floor. The ten-room suite also was equipped with a private elevator which provided ready access to the hotel's kitchen, so that when O.P. and M.J. wanted dinner, it could be whisked to their private dining room in quick order.

The multi-level suite originally contained sleeping rooms, a dining facility, and a spacious great room with vaulted ceiling, balcony, and fireplace. As they had chosen for their offices above, the Vans selected rich oak paneling from the Sherwood Forest for the walls of the great room.

After the deaths of the brothers, the suite was fortunately maintained and then subsequently leased by C&O Railroad. The railroad used the suite as a private hospitality center where the railroad's controversial chairman Cyrus Eaton often held court. The sleeping rooms were converted to additional dining space, and food was prepared in the suite's own kitchen. The private elevator to the hotel remained in place, but it was no longer used.

In 1975, C&O called in renowned interior decorator Carlton Varney to refurbish the facility. His work was faithful to the original design, and while modernizing its amenities and restoring its surfaces to like-new condition, he filled the den with antiques from the Van Sweringen era and a collection of other furnishings gathered from around the world. A modern security system was installed to protect the space from intruders.

After several mergers, the C&O eventually emerged as part of the CSX System, and in December 1986 it vacated

This dramatic view from track level of the lighted Terminal Tower helps explain why the Tower became such a meaningful symbol of the city for Greater Clevelanders. (Cleveland *Press* Collection of the Cleveland State University Libraries)

When the Tower first opened, its upper stories were floodlighted, with beacons from the 44th floor piercing the nighttime sky. (Cleveland *Press* Collection of the Cleveland State University Libraries)

The great room of the Van's private suite was richly paneled. The ten-room suite later became known at the Greenbrier Suite after it was leased by the Chesapeake and Ohio Railroad. The picture dates from that era. (Herbert H. Harwood Collection)

The Van Sweringens' private suite dining room after it was refurbished following the end of World War II. (Herbert H. Harwood Collection)

the Terminal Tower and relocated to new headquarters in Richmond, Virginia, and Jacksonville, Florida. The Greenbrier Suite then lay empty for six years until it was leased by the Walter, Haverfield, Buescher and Chockley law firm. Under the new proprietors the suite once again was refurbished and served the law firm as a conference center. After the law firm moved to larger offices in the Tower at Erieview, Forest City Enterprises took over the Tower's twelfth floor for its own use. The company will continue the tradition of using the Greenbrier Suite as a meeting and conference area.

Over the years the Greenbrier Suite served as an ideal venue to host prominent guests. Among the most famous of its visitors were the Duke and Duchess of Windsor, General Dwight D. Eisenhower, and President Harry S. Truman.

The Portico, the observation deck, and the Greenbrier Suite are among the more interesting features of the Terminal Tower. The building, however, was built primarily as an office facility, and that remains its chief use to this day.

From the very beginning, Tower management had no problem leasing the building's 582,000 square feet of space. It was, after all, Cleveland's most prestigious office building. The first tenant, the Van Sweringen's Cleveland Terminals Building Company, moved into the Tower in January 1927, while construction was still underway. Today, the Tower is the head-quarters for Forest City Enterprises, which is also its major tenant. The company's previous home was on Brookpark Road. It moved some offices to the Tower in 1991, and completed its headquarters relocation there in 1997. Other tenants include three primary civic organizations: the Greater Cleveland Partnership (formerly the Growth Association), the Downtown Cleveland Partnership, and the Convention and Visitors Bureau of Greater Cleveland, as well as law firms, realtors, investment offices, architects, and various types of business consultants. The Van Sweringen brothers' old offices on the 36th floor are now home to another venerable Cleveland firm, Picklands Mather and Company.

Keeping the building in good condition for its tenants and for the visiting public is the task of the Tower's owners and management. After the financial collapse of the Vans' empire, the Tower, operated by the Cleveland Terminals Building Company, went through a period of nearly 12 years during which the financial organization was completely reworked.

Between 1950 and 1964, the Tower's ownership changed hands five times. With the uncertainties that existed during the early years of reorganization and through the later years of frequent changes in ownership, there was some reluctance to provide the Tower with the full range of preventive maintenance services that might have been desirable.

The situation began to change in 1964 when Cleveland-based U. S. Realty Investments bought the Tower for $12.1 million. In 1968 the company also took over direct control of Tower management, which had previously been overseen from New York City.

Along with local control of the Terminal Tower, local pride and vision returned to play their parts once again in the building's revitalization. Many improvements in the physical plant were undertaken. Ceilings were lowered throughout the building. New air conditioning and electrical systems were installed. The portico was refurbished. A four-year program of exterior cleaning removed decades of accumulated grime, and tuck-pointing renewed the surface joints.

When the Tower was new, floodlights on the 44th and 48th floors illuminated the building's crown, but that practice ended with the restrictions that came with World War II. In 1974 U.S. Realty restored the lighting on the Tower's upper stories, but critics were not happy with the effect, one

This postcard view of the relighted Terminal Tower shows it as the brightest spectacle in the downtown Cleveland skyline. (Cleveland Landmarks Press Collection)

Keeping the Tower lighted could be a dizzying task. Here two workers, precariously perched on the 48th floor ledge, change lamps in the building's floodlights, 1936. (Blaine Hays Collection)

critic calling it "more crass than class." USRI took the criticism seriously and went back to the drawing boards. On the evening of July 13, 1981, a crowd of about 7,000 Clevelanders gathered on Public Square to witness the relighting of the Tower. Cleveland Mayor George Voinovich and Council President George Forbes shared the honor of throwing the switch. The result was spectacular; the entire Tower was bathed in a warm golden glow. Since 2001, to mark the Christmas holiday season, the Tower has taken on a different hue. Its usual golden tones are replaced by the traditional red and green of the season.

In January 1982 U. S. Realty Investments formally announced that it was going to liquidate its holdings. Forest City

Enterprises, which had been the Tower's part-owner since 1974, became the sole owner in October 1982 when it bought U. S. Realty's share. With the Tower and the Station then both under Forest City management, work on the Tower City Center project moved into high gear. Upgrading the Tower continued, and the office building was completely renovated in 1990. Beginning in 1992 Forest City Enterprises commissioned work to correct the deterioration which decades of harsh winters had inflicted on the building's limestone and terra cotta facing.

For 75 years the Tower has stood as Cleveland's proudest and most beloved symbol. As the city's central focal point, many events have taken place in, on, and in the shadow of the grand building. The years have contributed to a minor accumulation of Terminal Tower lore.

One frequently told story is about the ghost of the Terminal Tower. Some years ago, as building inspectors were walking through part of the third floor mechanical area, there loomed before them what appeared to be the body of a man. Recovering from their shock, they approached more closely to investigate. What they found was the legacy of a construction-era prank. Apparently workers at the time had taken the coveralls from one of their colleagues, filled them with concrete, and stationed them in the dimness. The coveralls have since disintegrated, and as a result, the now naked "ghost" has lost its fearsome character. But the clump of concrete remains.

It was on August 18, 1927, that the U. S. flag first flew from the Terminal Tower's flagpole, and it has done so for most of the years since. Hoisting the flag above the Tower was no easy task. It took two men. First they had to climb ten flights to arrive at the portal at the base of the flagpole. There one man would exit onto a narrow metal grating and attach the flag to the ropes as the other worker handed it out to him. In the brisk winds that often buffeted the upper reaches of the building, it was not a task for the timid. Testimony to the severity of the winds is that in bad weather, a flag would last only ten days.

The flag disappeared from the Tower's mast in 1972 when the flagpole was reconfigured as a radio antenna for a local

station. The tradition of flying the flag (along with the banners — depending on the season — of the Cleveland Browns or Indians beneath it) was restored in 1986 when the station built a new transmitting tower in the suburbs.

The Tower has another association with baseball. In 1938 the Tower was the scene for setting the world record for a high altitude baseball catch. Two members of the Cleveland Indians baseball team, Henry Helf and Frank Pytlak, were stationed in

The statue of Moses Cleaveland is dwarfed by the Tower. The statue and the Tower also form the backdrop for many of the city's festive events. (Greg Deegan photo)

The weather inevitably has its way with skyscrapers, requiring ongoing surface repair work. Here the Terminal Tower's upper floors get some attention. (J. A. Toman photo)

Public Square to catch a baseball tossed by teammate Kenny Keltner from the very top of the Tower. The first few balls Keltner dropped attained a velocity of 202 feet per second. Hitting the pavement, they bounced upwards some 13 stories. Undaunted, the baseball players "hung in there" until each had made a catch, to the cheers of some 10,000 well-wishing onlookers who crowded the Square.

The Terminal Complex celebrated its 50th anniversary with a week of parties and events in June 1980. Tens of thousands of Clevelanders made their way downtown to enjoy "parties in the park" in the Tower's Public Square front lawn, to ride up to the observation deck, to take in some of the planned stunts, or simply to revisit an old friend.

One of those stunts involved an attempt to replicate the 1938 baseball catch, but the 1980 version involved dropping a softball from the 52nd floor perch. This time the event did not turn out quite as smoothly. Ted Stepien, owner of the Cleveland Competitors professional soft-ball team, was stationed 700 feet above the street, and team members were arrayed along the Public Square roadway. The first toss flew all the way to Superior Avenue where it struck a car. The second toss was closer to target, but it struck the shoulder of an onlooker in the crowd gathered in the Square. The third toss broke the wrist of a young woman who had been stationed on the sidewalk opposite the Tower. The fourth toss hit the pavement and bounced some 40 feet into the air. Finally, on the fifth throw, Competitor outfielder Mike Zarefoss snared the toss. That ended the bombardment.

Another event that took place during the Golden Anniversary celebration involved Hollywood stunt man William deRoyer carrying out a rope descent from the top of the Tower. On June 27 a crowd of 5,000 gathered to watch the daring feat. The first part of his descent he performed as a sitting rappel. This brought him uneventfully to the 18th floor level. There he chose to swing out and continue the trip facing down to the sidewalk. As he was switching positions, his brakes failed, and he found himself spinning out into space. As the crowd held their collective breath, he regained control and made it safely to the ground. DeRoyer claimed the feat set a record: the Tower was the tallest building ever to be descended by rope.

The urban Tower became the atypical focus for naturalists beginning in 1993 when a pair of peregrine falcons made a nest on a 12th floor ledge. Because the species had once been listed on the endangered list, it was exciting to have a nesting pair choose the Tower location where their behavior patterns could be easily monitored. A "FalconCam" recorded the pair's every move, and the media gave Clevelanders regular updates on the falcons' comings and goings and of the battles fought in the downtown skies over the periodic challenges an interloper posed to the domestic peace of the nesting pair. In 2004, the current nest mates, Buckeye and SW, presided over the hatching of three chicks there.

Sometimes people ask if anyone ever attempted suicide from the Tower's

heights. It happened just once. One man leapt from a window of the 42nd observation deck floor. He landed on the protruding ledge of the floor below. Dazed, but not seriously injured by his short fall and perhaps reassessing what fate held in store for him, he was coaxed back into the building by members of the Tower's security staff.

There have been a few bizarre events in the Tower's history. In 1935 there was an apparent attempt to blow up the building. A homemade bomb, containing six sticks

The Terminal Tower was the central focus in celebrations to welcome the new millennium at midnight December 31, 1999. The giant light bulb burst into light when the clock struck midnight. (J. A. Toman photo)

91

of dynamite, was discovered by a tenant. The fuse had fizzled. Neither the perpetrator, nor his or her motive, was ever discovered. Another unsolved mystery occurred when an axe was either dropped or hurled from the Tower's upper heights. The axe plummeted towards Public Square, crashing through the windshield of an automobile parked in front of the building's main entrance. There were three occupants in the car at the time. All of them miraculously escaped serious injury.

Happily, the Terminal Tower is usually the backdrop for happier and more meaningful events. Since 1987 it has been the scene of the city's New Year's Eve celebrations, with fireworks set off from the Tower's 14th floor roof top. In 1990, to mark the Terminal's 60th anniversary, the Cleveland Orchestra performed a concert from a stage set up in front of the Tower's portico. An estimated 85,000 attended the event. The Cleveland Orchestra per-

formance proved so popular that it has become a yearly event. In 1995 thousands of Indians' fans gathered in front of the Tower to cheer the team on its way to its first World Series appearance in 41 years. In 1996 to mark the city's bicentennial, an 8 x 8 foot bicentennial logo was suspended from the Tower's 34th floor. For the New Year's Eve celebration to welcome in the new millenium, a display in the form of an 88-foot light bulb made up of 10,000 individual lights was affixed to the Public Square facade of the Terminal Tower. The bulb burst into light as the clock struck midnight. A crowd of 100,000 joined in the celebration.

And the list could go on.

What this short list means, though, is that for 75 years, the Terminal Tower has been the place where Clevelanders have chosen to gather to celebrate their city's heritage. No other venue could possibly compete.

Viewing the Christmas lights on Public Square, with the Terminal Tower as the backdrop, has long been a Cleveland tradition. (Cleveland *Press* Collection of the Cleveland State University Libraries)

As it marks its 75th anniversary, the Terminal Tower no longer dominates the Cleveland skyline, but its majesty has not been eclipsed by its taller and more massive rivals. (David Kachinko photo)

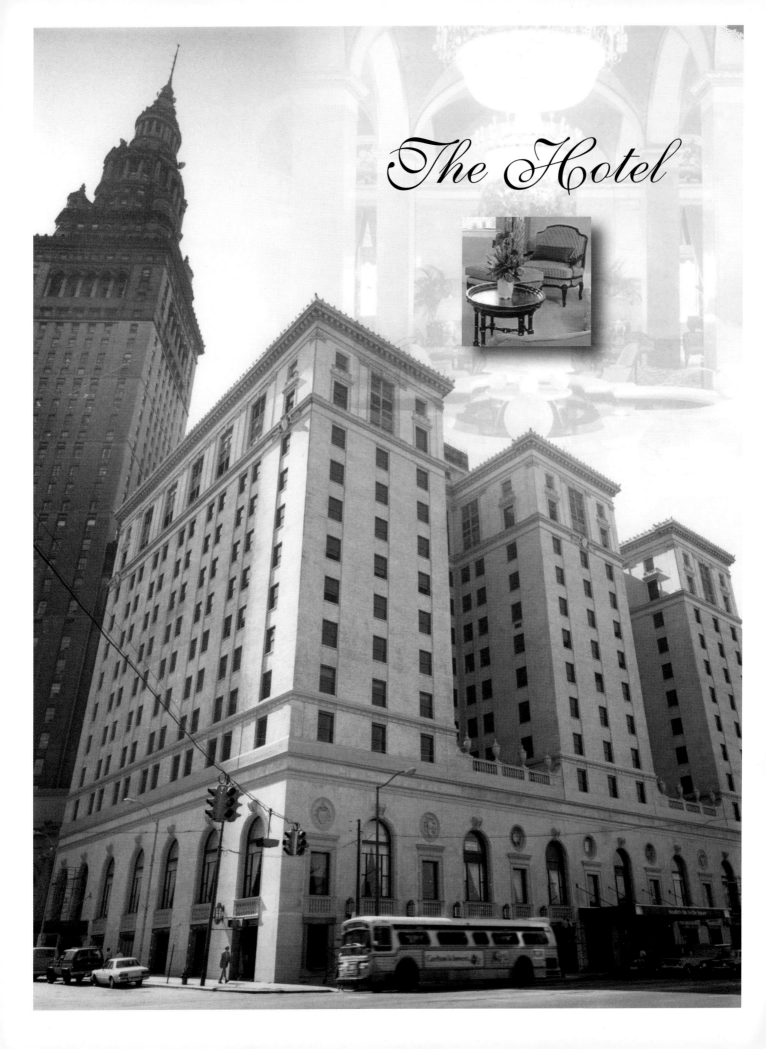

The Hotel

chapter 5

The Hotel Cleveland celebrated its grand opening on December 16, 1918. It was the first building in the planned Terminal complex to be completed. The reason that it came first was probably due to the Van Sweringen brothers' uncanny marketing skills. Clevelanders had been hearing about the Group Plan for a new Union Depot on the lakefront since 1903, but nothing had come of it. Then the Vans introduced their scheme for a Public Square station. The decision over the competing sites for the new railroad facility was to be made by the voters. Building the grand hotel on Public Square was the Vans' way of saying to the electorate: "Some talk; we perform." The hotel was a dramatic way of getting their point across. The celebrations that marked the hotel's opening were still fresh in the minds of voters when they went to the polls only three weeks later and gave the Vans their solid ballot-box victory.

The southwest corner of Public Square at Superior Avenue has long been the location for hotel facilities. From almost the founding days of the city, the site has been occupied by buildings devoted to serving the weary and hungry traveler. It was in 1815 that Phinney Mowrey, having invested $100 for a parcel of land at the corner of Public Square and Superior Avenue, began construction on a log structure that was to serve as a combination tavern and lodging house. Located across Superior Avenue from the city's first Court House, Mowrey had found a good location that would gain for his business a steady stream of thirsty customers.

Five years later the land and lodge changed hands for $4,500, and Mowrey's Tavern became Cleveland House.

From 1852 until 1915, the Forest City House occupied the southwest corner of Public Square and Superior Avenue. It was razed to make way for the Hotel Cleveland. (Bruce Young Collection)

Business continued to be brisk, and soon it became apparent that the existing structure was too small for the business it was drawing. In 1832 the old building was torn down, and a larger three-story Cleveland House was erected in its place. That building lasted until 1845 when it was destroyed by fire.

David Dunham then bought the land and erected a still larger hotel, this time made of brick, which he named the Dunham House. Business continued to prosper, and an addition was joined to the four-story structure in 1850.

In 1852 the prospering hotel was enlarged once again and, under new management, was renamed the Forest City House. By this time the hotel was not only a popular resting place for the traveler but also a favorite gathering spot for Clevelanders. Its dining and meeting facilities hosted many assemblies of civic and political leaders.

The Forest City House phase in the property's history was both long and distinguished. It was the hotel where

Hotel Cleveland was the first of the Terminal Complex structures to be completed. A streetcar pulling a trailer passes the hotel on its way to the Detroit-Superior bridge subway. (Cleveland Landmarks Press Collection)

Opening night came on December 16, 1918. The mezzanine ballroom hosted a crowd of 1,500 who celebrated the event. (Cleveland Landmarks Press Collection)

presidents stayed and where many Cleveland organizations were born. The Forest City House era lasted for 63 years.

As always when an era comes to an end, there was sadness in the city when the aging hotel closed its doors for the last time on September 16, 1915. As faithful as Forest City House's service had been, Cleveland's growing prosperity and prominence in the world of industry and commerce made a larger and more modern downtown hotel facility a necessity. The Van Sweringen brothers were waiting in the wings to deliver.

The Vans' Terminal Hotels Company (the name foreshadowed the future station development) purchased the land from its former owners in July 1916, and the old structure was torn down. For an investment of $4.5 million, a thousand times more than was required to build the predecessor Cleveland House almost a century earlier, the new Hotel Cleveland rose on the site.

The architect for the new hotel was Graham, Anderson, Probst & White. The general contractor was the Thompson-Starret Company. Rising 14 stories, the gleaming light-grey building was faced with granite for the first three stories, and with brick and terra cotta on the floors above. On its Superior Avenue frontage, the hotel was shaped like the letter "E." The rear portion of the hotel was built around an interior light well. The architects had decided this was the optimum way to assure that every one of the 1,000 guest rooms could boast of a window and benefit from natural lighting. The windows, of course, were also of particular value during this era preceding the invention of air-conditioning.

The hotel also boasted of many amenities. The ground floor level hosted two restaurants, the Bronze Room and the Lunch Room, as well as a cigar stand, barber shop, and billiard room. Another dining area, the Rose Room, was located on the main floor. A ballroom, two assembly rooms, a lounge, and a flower shop occupied the mezzanine level. Private dining rooms and a conference suite were on the next floor up, which the hotel called its "parlor floor."

After a little more than two years of construction, the new Hotel Cleveland was ready to open. Its debut came on December 16, 1918, to a city still celebrating

The area immediately to the west of Hotel Cleveland was one of the parcels which the Van Sweringens had hoped to develop. The onset of the Depression put an end to those plans, 1929. (Cleveland Picture Collection of Cleveland Public Library)

the end of the World War I. A giant civic reception for 1,500 guests marked the event, and the new building's dining facilities were given their first major test. The reaction of the throng was everything the Vans could have hoped for. The distinguished guests marveled over the spacious and elegant lobby and were delighted by the wonderful view of Public Square its windows afforded (the lobby is situated one level above the street entrances).

The new hotel experienced immediate success, one that only increased when Cleveland Union Terminal opened for passenger business in 1930. Railroad travelers were pleased by the convenience

The major change which the Sheraton Hotel chain brought to the hotel came in 1962, a new parking garage and ballroom. Sheraton hoped the new facility would boost the sagging fortunes of the hotel. (Greater Cleveland Growth Association)

The new ballroom/banquet hall was the largest facility of its kind between New York City and Chicago. (Cleveland Landmarks Press Collection)

the hotel offered. Alighting from their trains, they simply had to pass along the concourse level of the station and up one of the ramps that led to the Public Square level. A turn to the left brought them right to the doors of the hotel. There was no need for a taxi; the traveler was spared from having to face the uncertain prospects of Cleveland's weather.

After the Vans' empire collapsed, the Hotel Corporation of America took over the operation of the hotel. Then, in 1958, the property was turned over to the Sheraton Hotel chain, and its name changed to the Sheraton Cleveland Hotel.

By the time of the Sheraton takeover, the hotel was facing some problems. With the decline of the passenger railroad trade, the hotel's claim on convenience was no longer a guarantee of a robust occupancy rate. The size of the guest rooms had also become problematic. Lodgers, who had at one time been accustomed to the confined spaces of trains' passenger compartments, were now looking for hotel rooms that were more spacious and comfortable. The new owners also recognized that the hotel's existing dining-banquet hall facilities were too small to host major gatherings.

With high hopes, the Sheraton people poured money into renovating the 40-year old building. Room size was enlarged, leading to a reduction in their number from the original 1,000 to 758. The top floor of the hotel was converted to commercial office space, and the entire facility received air-conditioning. Decidedly less appealing was the decision to remodel the lobby, the result of which was that the

The 1977-1978 renovation of the hotel gave it a new marquee and a new name, Stouffer's Inn on the Square. (Stouffer's Hotels photo, Cleveland Landmarks Press collection)

Work gets under way during the Stouffer renovations to create an atrium to replace the old interior light court. (Stouffer's Hotels photo, Cleveland Landmarks Press collection)

boxlike style then popular, the National Register of Historic Places decided that it did "not intrude excessively on the character of the whole group." The renovations carried a price tag of $5.2 million and were completed in December 1962. One of Sheraton's most popular new attractions was the Kon Tiki, a Polynesian restaurant located on the Superior level. Exotic in both decor and menu, the Kon Tiki was a favorite destination for prom night festivities and graduation parties.

Despite the investment, the Sheraton Cleveland continued to face difficult times. Just a few blocks east on Superior Avenue, the new Hollenden House opened in 1965. In 1970 the Bond Court Hotel, situated next to the Cleveland Convention Center, made its appearance. It later became the next downtown home for the Sheraton chain. These new downtown hotels offered stiff competition, as did the several new hotels and motels being opened near the Cleveland Hopkins International Airport and along the interstate highways that entered the city.

As revenues began to decline, a series of complaints appeared in the news media about the hotel, alleging that its housekeeping practices were not up to par. In 1971 the Cleveland Health Department ordered Sheraton Cleveland management to improve sanitary conditions on the premises. The bad publicity led to a further decline in the fortunes of the hotel.

In 1975 the Sheraton chain sold the hotel to Cleveland Tower Hotel, Inc., a group headed by investor Thomas Lloyd. At the time of the sale, plans were announced for a major renovation of the facility, but that was not to be. Affairs went

rich detail of the original was covered over by a bland form of modernism.

The major improvement, however, was the construction of a new banquet hall/ballroom atop a three-level parking garage adjoining the hotel at its western end. The need for more parking had become acute since the principal mode of intercity travel had shifted away from the railroads. The banquet facility, the largest of its kind between New York City and Chicago, was seen as a means of attracting new business to the hotel. Although the ballroom addition was designed in the from bad to worse, occupancy fell to only 12%, and bankruptcy soon followed. The property went into receivership in November 1976. It was a tremendous blow to the city, another in a series of setbacks that seemed to give evidence that Cleveland was in a downward spiral.

It was at this point that an event took place which probably was more significant than simply the issue of the hotel's fate. Judge John Patton appointed his friend Art Modell, president of the Cleveland Browns football team and head of the Stadium Corporation, as the hotel's receiver. Modell then sought out a group of fellow Clevelanders who would work together to rescue the hotel. The team he assembled included F. J. O'Neill, the Stouffer Corporation, the Higbee Company, Eaton Corporation, TRW, Inc., the Chessie System, the Diamond Shamrock Corporation, as well as Modell's own Stadium Corporation. Each member of the group committed $1 million to the project, which made possible another $9 million secured through a loan from Central National Bank. At a sheriff's sale, the group purchased the facility for $4 million. On August 1, 1977, the hotel closed, and the task of renovation began.

Cleveland-based Stouffer Corporation became the operating partner in the group. Under Stouffer leadership (no newcomer to the hotel business, Stouffer's operated 20 hotels around the country), $14 million was put into the restoration project. John Stauffer was named project manager. As the hotel neared its 60th birthday, it was poised for a total transformation.

The group had decided on a total renovation of the building rather than a cosmetic retouching. The renewal of the building's exterior is what caught the attention of passers by. The hotel's facade was steam cleaned and tuckpointed. Sixty years of accumulated grime gave way to a fresh, clean light-grey finish. Old windows throughout the facility were removed. The replacements not only provided greater energy efficiency, they also added a richer tone to the building's exterior.

The Superior Avenue entrance, with its grand stairway, had been intended as the building's main entrance, but traffic patterns over the years had made it more convenient for guests to enter from the Public Square side. To change that pattern, a drive-up accessway was cut into the sidewalk on the hotel's Superior Avenue frontage, and an

When the renovations were complete, the hotel had lost 60 years of grime and soot. It looks much brighter than its neighboring Terminal Tower, which had not yet received its surface cleaning. (Stouffer's Hotels photo, Cleveland Landmarks Press collection)

The stately lobby of the hotel was returned to its original configuration as part of the renovations in the late 70s. (Renaissance Hotels)

On the upper floors, the guest rooms were totally remodeled. With an emphasis on space and comfort, the former 758 rooms were further reduced in number to 520, among which were 38 luxuriously appointed two-room suites. Each room received new carpeting, wall coverings, furniture, and lavatory facilities.

The 24 meeting rooms were also renovated. The Grand Ballroom, which can hold 2,500 people for a banquet or seat 3,500 in theatre-style chairs for a meeting, was extensively reburbished. Commercial space was kept at a minimum, relegated only to the lower level. The top floor of the hotel remained an office facility.

The most intriguing feature of the renovation was the enclosure of the hotel's interior light well. That dingy space was converted into a skylighted atrium, stretching from the fifth through the tenth floors. The architects positioned reflecting panels on the atrium walls to accentuate the dimensions of the area. For the large number of the guest rooms facing onto the atrium, the once unsightly space became an inviting vista. From their rooms, guests could look down at the lounge with its swimming pool and bar. Rooms on the fifth floor were given small patios.

A classy restaurant, the French Connection, was located right off the main lobby, and two more dining areas, Mowrey's (named after the first inn on the site) and the Brasserie were built on the Superior Avenue level.

The Stouffer Corporation had not only taken the lead in overseeing the restoration project, it had also agreed to manage the refurbished hotel. As a result, the hotel gained a new name, Stouffer's Inn on the Square.

attractive skylighted bronze-toned marquee was installed.

The hotel lobby, totaling 9,200 square feet, was totally redone. In place of the shops which had ringed the room, the designer inserted a continental style café and liberally used ferns and floral arrangements throughout. New wall coverings were added, the supporting columns regained their rich marble veneer, crystal chandeliers sparkled above, and plush carpeting and comfortable furniture created an inviting atmosphere. The lobby once again exuded an atmosphere of quiet elegance.

Although the entire renovation project had not yet been completed, Stouffer's Inn on the Square opened to the public on September 22, 1978. As had been the case when the old Hotel Cleveland first opened in 1918, the re-opening was cause for a celebration. Some 2,000 guests attended the inaugural festivities. An important part of downtown Cleveland had not only been rescued from bankruptcy, it once again emerged as a showcase for what was right about the city. The renovation won the applause of the American Automobile Association which gave the renovated facility its Four Star rating.

The restored hotel not only was favorably received by the traveler, it also became a popular destination for the Greater Clevelanders interested in a change of pace. Stouffer's aggressively marketed the hotel to the local population, touting its amenities in a package that it called "L'Esprit Weekend." The Inn on the Square package included an overnight stay, dinner at the French Connection, champagne, breakfast in bed, and, of course, the amenities of the Atrium facilities.

Stouffer's did not rest on its laurels. Over the next dozen years, it spent another $35 million on further improvements to the facility, which included a health club and fitness center and further meeting and guest room redecoration. The hotel also received a new name, Stouffer Tower City Plaza Hotel, to better identify it with the changes taking place in the adjoining Terminal Complex buildings.

Stouffer Corporation, a Cleveland-based company founded in 1922, was a respected presence in the local community.

Its restaurant, hotel, and frozen food divisions had all shown significant growth, and the company developed into a national presence. Then in 1973, Stouffer's was taken over by the Nestle Corporation, and operated as a division of Nestle. By the mid-1980s Nestle was immersed in a process of reexamining its business operations. The result was that it decided to sell its restaurant and hotel divisions and to concentrate on its core food-product lines.

In March 1993 Nestle sold the 40 properties operated by its Stouffer Hotels and Resorts Division to Cheng Yu-Tang, a Hong Kong businessman whose New World Development Company was then operating a worldwide network of 96 hotels bearing the Renaissance label. The hotel thus gained a new owner, but it continued to operate under the Stouffer name. That changed on May 16, 1996, when a bottle of champagne was smashed against the building's Superior facade, and it was rechristened the Renaissance Cleveland Hotel.

Plans for a 19-story guest-room annex were announced in 1994. The addition would have been fitted into the open triangle of land formed by the intersection of Superior and Prospect avenues. (Cleveland Landmarks Press Collection)

The Renaissance Cleveland has continually upgraded the hotel property; its 491 rooms and suites are regularly refurbished and always well appointed. (Renaissance Hotels)

eliminated one of the two remaining gaps in the original Van Sweringen site plans. The addition was to be ready by 1996, but in 1997, with the Renaissance Hotels about to become a part of the Marriott Hotel chain (which already was operating two hotels in downtown Cleveland), the plan was scrapped.

Although the Renaissance Cleveland Hotel became a part of Marriott Hotels, Marriott decided to continue operating its newly gained property under the Renaissance name. The first major change under the new ownership was to return the top floor from leased office space to guest use. That came about in 1997.

Under Renaissance management, the hotel has continued to receive excellent care. An ongoing commitment to keep the hotel a Four Star operation has seen a pattern of regular renovation of its current guest rooms and meeting halls; in 2003 the hotel spent $5.5 million to refurbish all 491

While still under Stouffer management, plans were drawn up for a major addition to the hotel. The plan, as devised by Bojtos Architects of Cleveland called for a 362-room, 19-story annex which would rise on the surface parking area to the west of the ballroom. The construction would have

The mezzanine level of the Renaissance Cleveland Hotel continues the opulent appointments found in the main-floor lobby area. (Renaissance Hotels)

of its guest rooms and suites. The lobby-level Sans Souci Restaurant has consistently been rated at the top or near the top of Cleveland's fine dining rooms.

Over the years, the hotel with several names has been the gathering place for many events of local importance. It has played host to many of the nation's political leaders and celebrities. Among them have been Presidents Harry S. Truman, Richard Nixon, and Ronald Reagan, who have spoken from its podium, as have the Rev. Martin Luther King, Jr., Charles Lindbergh, and comedian Bob Hope. The variety of events that it has hosted has ranged from the banquet for the Rock and Roll Hall of Fame induction ceremony to the Cleveland Thanksgiving Polka Party. It has been the site for countless wedding celebrations and prom nights.

Besides its debt to the forward-thinking Van Sweringen brothers, the Renaissance Cleveland Hotel shares another distinction with the Vans' development to its south, the old Cleveland Union Terminal. Not too long ago, both seemed to have outlived their usefulness, and it appeared that their time of greatness had passed. But, as was true for the station, those who were ready to write the hotel's epitaph were premature. While mediocre buildings succumb to the ravages of time, great buildings survive.

After 87 years of operation, the Renaissance Cleveland Hotel continues its proud history. It can face the future with confidence.

The Sans Souci restaurant on the hotel's lobby level is a favorite dining place for those seeking a comfortable setting, fine food, and excellent service. (Renaissance Hotels)

Prospect Buildings to
Landmark Office Towers

chapter 6

Chances are that when Greater Clevelanders hear the name "Prospect Buildings," they will be puzzled. Perhaps they might visualize the rowhouses along upper Prospect Avenue or perhaps they might think of some of the structures that line the lower avenue between Ontario and East Ninth streets. Relatively few, though, would likely link the "Prospect Buildings" name to the giant structure located between Prospect Avenue and Huron Road, between Ontario and West Second streets. Nor would most of them readily recognize that what appears to be one large structure is actually three separate buildings. These separate structures were originally named the Medical Arts, Builders Exchange, and Midland buildings. Even the current name for the complex, Landmark Office Towers, is unlikely to ring a bell.

As important as this giant office structure has been to the business life of the city, it has never had the public profile which the other elements in the Terminal Complex have had.

The relative unfamiliarity of the Prospect Buildings to the Cleveland public is due to their nature as office facilities. They have few of the attractions for the

Exterior work is moving along on the Medical Arts Building, while steel work continues on the Builders Exchange Building, April 1929. (Cleveland Union Terminal Archives of the Cleveland State University Libraries)

general public that distinguish their partners in the Terminal Complex. This does not diminish, however, the significant role that the buildings have played in the economic life of the city. The Prospect Buildings have a long and distinguished history as the headquarters of some of the city's major corporations.

The Prospect Buildings were an integral part of the air rights design of the Terminal Complex. Built between the Prospect

Prospect Buildings to the East Traction Concourse of Cleveland Union Terminal. This feature made the neighboring department store and the restaurants and shops of the station area easily accessible to workers and patrons of the office block and helps to explain why those kinds of commercial features were largely absent from the Prospect Buildings.

Three in number, the Prospect Buildings appear at first glance to be a single structure. The three buildings are joined together and share the same architectural style. A closer examination, however, reveals that each has its own distinctive ornamental detail. Architect for the three buildings was, once again, the firm of Graham, Anderson, Probst & White. The firm claimed that the design for the office block would "be free of any suggestion of historic period or style." Instead, the buildings would emphasize their vertical elements, and by using corner

The first two of the Prospect Buildings are substantially finished, but work has yet to begin on the Midland Building. An advertisement for the "home in the sky" temporarily covers the wall soon to be covered by construction on the Midland Building. (Cleveland Union Terminal Archives of the Cleveland State University Libraries)

Avenue, Huron Road, and West Second Street bridges and above the eastern track entrance to the Cleveland Union Terminal, the buildings were intended to maximize the Van Sweringens' real estate income. An underground passage connected the

The architects believed that the eight-story recesses on the western frontage of the Midland Building would help reduce the massive appearance of the building. (Jack Muslovski photo, Cleveland Landmarks Press Collection)

setbacks on the top floor would present "a broken skyline, forming an interesting silhouette." Graham, Anderson, Probst & White called the approach "Modern American Architecture." Unlike their design for the Terminal Tower, which reflects an earlier beaux arts style, the architects decided that the Prospect Buildings would instead reflect features from the contemporary art deco movement.

The Van Sweringens' Cleveland Terminals Building Company was responsible for the project. In 1928 construction began on the first of the buildings, the Medical Arts Building. The second edifice, the Builders Exchange Building, got underway later that same year. General contractor for both of these was the Lundoff-Bicknell Company of Cleveland and Chicago. The third building, the Midland Bank Building, was started one

year later. Its general contractor was the Aronberg-Fried Company of New York and Cleveland.

The structures are designed in a uniform 260-foot, 18-story height. A 19th floor setback holds mechanical equipment, and a 20th floor stainless steel penthouse was later added to the roof of Medical Arts Building. Faced with limestone, each building is ornamented in art deco style. The massiveness of the structure is countered by five eight-story recesses, three on the Huron Road and two on the West Second Street frontages. These also served as light courts, and provided ventilation in an era before air conditioning. A sixth light court, extending the full 18 stories, forms part of the Ontario Street frontage of the Medical Arts Building. One more light court was situated in the interior of the building.

The appearance of the Builders' Exchange building was affected by the use of recesses. These spaces also served a practical purpose, giving the massive building better ventilation and light. The view is of the Huron Road frontage. (J. A. Toman photo)

The most distinguished space in the Prospect Buildings was the Midland Arcade, the main banking room for the Midland Bank. (Cleveland Picture Collection of Cleveland Public Library)

The Prospect Avenue facade is solid. Because it follows the angle of the street, the Prospect vista appears longer than it really is. The massive complex contains 1.4 million square feet of space, of which 900,800 square feet is leaseable. The complex's size makes it Cleveland's fifth largest office building (following Key Tower, the Huntington Building, the BP Tower, and the Celebrezze Federal Office Building).

The architects' appreciation of the growing importance of the automobile is evidenced by their having included indoor garage space in the structure. Entered from Huron Road, the nine-story Terminal Garage originally had room for 1,300 automobiles. Each floor of the garage had direct access to the office building. When the garage first opened, it served the needs not only of the office tenants, but it also appealed to downtown shoppers since the connecting underground passageways gave them a climate-neutral route to The Higbee Company and the Harvey Shops.

As demand for office space grew, however, garage space was gradually reduced. Between 1953 and 1970 the garage's original nine floors were trimmed back to four floors. As the space was reduced, the convenience of the garage was reserved for the exclusive use of the leaseholders. The public was not

The only purpose the stubby rooftop structure atop the Builders Exchange Building served was to raise the ceiling of the 18th floor so the Home in the Sky could comfortably fit in the three-floor space allotted to it. (J. A. Toman photo)

unduly inconvenienced, however, as it was just about this time that the parking area immediately south of the Prospect Buildings' site (the former coach yards) was paved and converted to public parking use.

There have been other changes in the buildings as well. As its name indicated, the Medical Arts Building was conceived as a prime location for doctors' and dentists' offices. In 1936, however, a new major tenant was taken into the building. Republic Steel Corporation, then located in Youngstown, moved its corporate head-quarters to Cleveland and settled into the Medical Arts Building. In acknowledgment of its new corporate tenant, the building's name was changed in that same year, and it became known as the Republic Building. As Republic Steel's need for space increased, building management decided to meet it by not renewing leases for space then being used for medical offices. By the mid-1960s, the last of the doctors' offices had been vacated and the space converted for the use of the prime tenant.

In 1984 Republic Steel merged with Jones and Laughlin Steel Corporation and became known as LTV Steel. The Republic Building was then renamed the LTV Building until LTV Steel relocated to the BP Tower in 1996. The Republic name was then restored to the office tower.

The second of the Prospect Buildings to be erected, the Builders Exchange Building, was intended as a home for the construction industry. Its most prominent tenant was the Cleveland Builders Exchange; hence the name.

A feature of the building, quite popular with the general public, was the use of the

16th through 18th floors as an exhibit hall to spotlight developments in the building industry. Among the displays was a model home, dubbed the "Home in the Sky" because of its lofty setting. Designed by Fred J. Abendroth, the model home measured 56 feet by 51 feet, and was 35 feet tall. To accommodate the height of the house, the roof of the 18th floor had to be opened and the clearance extended. A modest addition was built over that space to provide a new roof line (that structure, no longer serving any purpose, remains in place to this day). The "Home in the Sky" was decorated and furnished by The May Company, whose descriptive booklet informed visitors to the display that "duplicates of all furnishings in this Home are on display in corresponding departments at our store." The display was a popular attraction for several years.

When the Builders Exchange relocated its offices in 1941, the building's name was changed to the Guildhall Building.

The tables are gone from the space long occupied by the Guildhall Restaurant. The room is about to be converted into a fitness center. (John Schillo photo)

Ress Realty managed the Prospect Buildings for many years and kept them in tip-top shape. A major renovation took place in 1982, giving the classic elevator lobbies a modern look. (John Schillo photo)

The 1982 renovations also created a combined lobby, and gave the entryway a contemporary feel with the liberal use of glass. (The Krill Company)

Another distinguished feature of the building was the 10th floor Guildhall Restaurant, with it main dining room, and its smaller Green, Grey, and Colonial rooms. The main dining room, with its solid silver service, was nestled below the interior light well and was suffused with natural light from a skylight fixed at the 11th floor level. The skylight was covered over during World War II.

The restaurant space was later converted into a fitness center.

The third building in the complex was designed to accommodate the headquarters of one of Cleveland's newer financial institutions, the Midland Bank. The bank was formed in 1921 by a group of businessmen with close associations with the Van Sweringen brothers. Taking advantage of the connection, the brothers persuaded the bank to move its headquarters into the new complex. The most famous feature of the Midland Building was its expansive and elegantly paneled main banking lobby. Its ornamental plaster ceiling was 33 feet in height. Unfortunately, the Midland Bank did not long occupy its sumptuous new setting. Weakened by the Depression, the bank turned to the Cleveland Trust Company to rescue it, and it was absorbed into Cleveland Trust in 1932. The building's Midland name, however, has remained.

Since Cleveland Trust had an intricately carved wood-paneled branch in the Medical Arts Building (that space is now occupied by First Merit), it had no need for the Midland space. As a result, the opulent banking lobby remained empty.

In 1949 the banking lobby finally received a new tenant. Central National Bank had decided to give up its former headquarters on Euclid Avenue near East Fourth Street to make way there for a new F. W. Woolworth Company store. Central National Bank relocated its headquarters to the Midland Building and remained there until 1970 when it moved once again, this time to its new tower at the corner of Superior Avenue and East Ninth Street (now the McDonald Investments Building).

During Central National Bank's years in the building, it determined that the space occupied by the expansive lobby could be better utilized for needed office space. In a process that brought pain to those who cherished the rich detail of the original lobby, the ornate ceiling was covered over, and the balcony level was converted to office uses. After its move, Central National Bank retained an branch office in the modified lobby. It advertised its Midland location via a gigantic sign on the top of the building which remained in place until 1985.

After Central National Bank's departure, the huge building's more than 900,000 square feet of space was fully occupied by only four tenants, three of which were numbered among Cleveland's largest and most successful industrial corporations, Standard Oil Company of Ohio (Sohio), Republic Steel Corporation, and Sherwin-Williams Company.

The Fortune 500 Standard Oil Company of Ohio was then Cleveland's largest industrial company. While it called the Midland Building its headquarters, its space was spread throughout the complex. Republic Steel Corporation, then America's seventh largest metals manufacturer and Cleveland's third largest industrial firm, was ranked 82nd on the Fortune 500. Sherwin-Williams, a major force in the United States chemicals industry and the city's seventh largest firm, held the 239th slot on the Fortune 500 list. The fourth tenant of the complex was the Erie-Lackawanna Railroad. While the railroad's operations had been merged into Conrail, the local Erie-Lackawanna office housed the trustees for the original road's assets and interests.

When the Van Sweringen enterprises collapsed in 1935, the buildings were purchased by an ownership group known as the Prospect Terminal Building Company. Later, ownership was transferred to 66 Trust of Philadelphia, a pension fund. At that time, the four major tenants of the complex got together to form a management firm to oversee the daily operations of their corporate homes. They named their new association Ress Realty (Ress is an acronym: "R" for Republic, "E" for Erie. and a twinned "S" for Sohio and Sherwin-Williams). Ress Realty then negotiated a lease with the building owner to assure that building upkeep and services matched the needs and expectations of the four tenants.

The Midland Arcade became the Van Sweringen Arcade in a careful 1986 restoration project. The ornate original ceiling was recreated, but a different lighting system was installed. (Landmark Office Towers Collection)

The former Midland Bank vault became the Haymarket Restaurant cocktail lounge in 1986. While it guaranteed a safe setting, it probably was not popular with the claustrophobic. (The Krill Company)

The tenant picture for the buildings remained intact until 1984 when Standard Oil of Ohio moved its headquarters operation to its new tower on Public Square (while it abandoned 300,000 square feet of space in the Prospect complex, it retained another 150,000 square feet of space there). Standard Oil later was purchased by British Petroleum, which in turn merged with Amoco. At that point BP-Amoco offices were centralized in Chicago. In 1996 LTV Steel left its Prospect Avenue home to move into the space BP had abandoned in its Public Square tower. Just a few years later,

however, LTV Steel was forced to seek bankruptcy protection, and most of the company's assets were taken over by the International Steel Group (ISG).

While it would not be intellectually tenable to suggest that leaving the Prospect Buildings was a jinx, at least in terms of corporate longevity, perhaps the culture of the Prospect Buildings exuded a stabilizing influence that helped promote Cleveland as a major corporate headquarters city.

The space abandoned by the moves of these major tenants did not remain empty very long. The well-maintained office building quickly welcomed a variety of new tenants, and happily in the complex's 75th anniversary year, it maintains an occupancy level of better than 90%.

There are several factors that have enabled the Prospect Buildings to continue as a success story for so many years. Naturally, the central location and excellent public transit facilities have played a major role. So too has convenient parking. But a more significant reason can be found in the structure's unique management arrangement which assured that the building was kept in excellent shape and regularly renovated to accommodate the changing needs of technology and shifting tastes in decor.

The pending departure of Sohio signaled that a more aggressive renovation of the property might be prudent. A series of changes took place beginning in 1982. Ress Realty hired the architectural firm of Tufts and Wenzel to create a new look for the building's entryways and lobbies. The Krill Company was the contractor. The project combined the three separate building lobbies into one, added a central stairway to connect with the passageway to Cleveland Union Terminal, and remodeled the exterior entranceways. The total effect was to replace the dated look of the entry areas with a fresh and modern appearance, with more glass and stainless steel for the central lobby. The lobby area also received a new ceiling, lighting, and flooring along with extensive plantings of shrubs and trees to complete the new look.

In 1985, the Prospect Buildings were renamed the Landmark Office Towers, and Sherwin-Williams Company, an occupant of the buildings since 1930 and one of the Ress partners, purchased the property

from its then current owner, Textron, Inc., of Providence, Rhode Island. Sherwin-Williams reaffirmed its commitment to the property and to its continuing renovation.

The most spectacular aspect of the Sherwin-Williams commitment was the restoration of the old Midland Bank lobby which had been so radically changed by Central National Bank. The

This sketch shows how the proposed Gateway at Landmark would have filled in one of the last remaining gaps from the Van Sweringen days. It would have been located at the corner of Huron road and Ontario Street. (Landmark Office Towers)

architect, Teare, Herman & Gibans, Inc., was given the charge to restore the lobby to its former splendor. The Krill Company was construction manager. The false ceiling and mechanical equipment that it hid were removed. The ornamental-plaster ceiling, which had been seriously damaged in the 1970 renovation, was repaired and repainted, and the room's English oak paneling and sculpted wood columns were restored. The first glimpse of the restored ceiling came in September 1985 when Cleveland Mayor George Voinovich presided over the unveiling. The completed lobby project, renamed the Van Sweringen Arcade in honor of the two brothers whose vision had brought the complex into existence, was dedicated on November 21, 1986.

The Arcade is the only facility in Cleveland to bear the name of the men whom Cleveland journalist George Condon called "the builders of modern Cleveland"

(cf. Condon in reference list). The Arcade is available for rental and has been a popular choice for wedding receptions.

The project also entailed creating space on the main floor of the Midland Building for a restaurant. The restaurant's bar was built into the old bank's safety deposit box vault, creating one of downtown's most interesting watering holes. The Haymarket was the first restaurant to occupy the space. The Haymarket was later followed by the Piperade, and then by the Hyde Park Grille. The vault space is no longer a bar. It was renovated into one of Hyde Park's three private dining areas.

In 1989 Sherwin-Williams announced plans for the Gateway at Landmark, a major addition to the Landmark Office Towers. The plan called for a dramatic 30-story tower to be built at the corner of Ontario Street and Huron Road, just across the street from the Gund Arena at Gateway. The proposed building would have filled another gap left open when the Van Sweringen plans were stymied by the Depression. Construction however, was contingent on finding an anchor tenant for the 600,000 square feet of space that the new building would contain. With the Society (now Key), Bank One (now Fifth-Third), and Skylight Office towers all then being developed, there was a glut of new downtown office space all arriving at about the same time. As a result the Gateway at Landmark development was pulled from the drawing board.

Other changes have continued to take place. The lobby was remodeled once again, this time in a more classic look with an emphasis on paneling. Brass was also restored to the building entrance way, in a style reminiscent of the original art deco design. The upper floors of the complex and the rooftop penthouse area were also extensively renovated as the new home for Wyse Advertising.

Over the years, astute management and meticulous maintenance have kept the Landmark Office Towers a highly desirable business address. And with such historic names as Sherwin-Williams and Van Sweringen deeply etched in the building's heritage, the tradition seems certain to continue.

The view of the Landmark Office Towers from the Key Tower conveys how Graham, Anderson, Probst & White managed to create a massive structure while still giving it a graceful profile, one that is perhaps more evident from a height than it is at street level. (J. A. Toman photo)

U. S. Post Office to MK-Ferguson Plaza

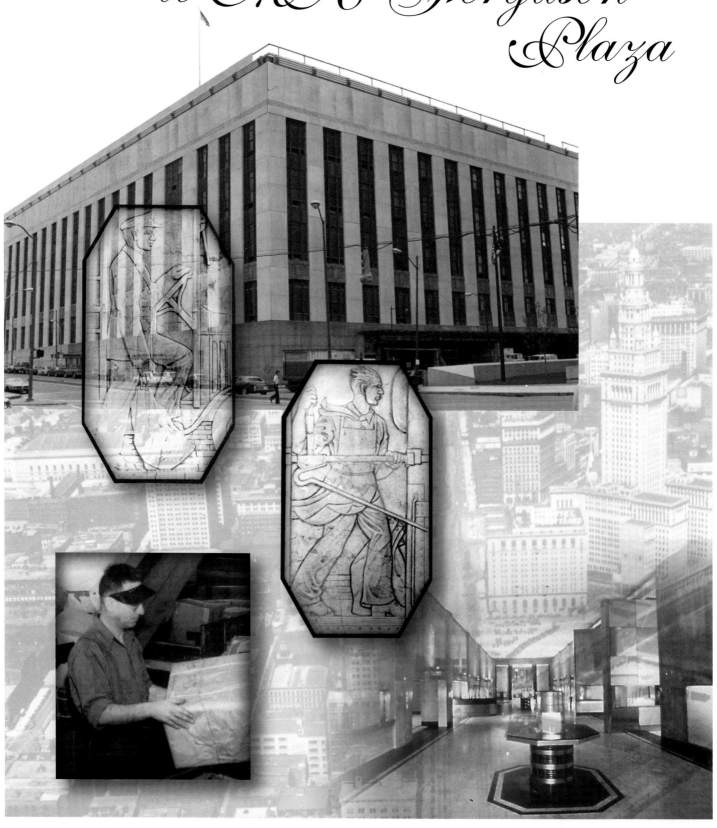

chapter 7

The last structure to be built in the Terminal Complex became the main headquarters of the Cleveland branch of the United States Post Office. The new building replaced the previous postal headquarters, the 1911 U.S. Post Office, Customs House and Court House, on the northeast corner of Superior Avenue and Public Square. The vacated space in the older building was re-allocated to other federal purposes.

In February 1932, construction began on the new main Post Office building, using a foundation put into place earlier as part of the overall Terminal Complex planning. Its site, occupying a total of 99,000 square feet, is bounded by Huron Road, Prospect Avenue, and West Third and West Sixth streets. As is true of the Landmark Office Towers, its neighbor to the east, the Post Office site was circumscribed by roadways built atop bridge structures.

The site for the new postal facility was an attractive one. The old Public Square main post office had been positioned without due regard for the importance of railroad access for the receipt and delivery

of the mails. Because the new building adjoined Cleveland Union Terminal, it was considered an ideal location.

As a federal facility, the Post Office was nominally designed under the guiding hand of official United States Architect, James A. Wetmore. For all practical purposes, however, it was the local partnering architects who were chiefly responsible for the design. The Cleveland firm of Walker & Weeks, in association with Philip L. Small, received the commission. At the time, Walker & Weeks was probably the city's most prestigious architectural firm. The partnership was responsible for, among others, the main Cleveland Public Library building, Public Auditorium, the Federal Reserve Bank of Cleveland Building, the Superior Building, Cleveland Municipal Stadium, and Severance Hall. The Post Office building was the only member of the Terminal Group designed by a local firm. For it, the architects chose a subdued art deco style. The Lundoff-Bicknell Company was the general contractor.

Since the Post Office was built as a government facility and at federal

Construction work continues on the Huron Road bridge structure. The West Sixth Street bridge is completed, as is the roadway leading to the lower level of the future post office site. (Robert Runyon photo, Bruce Young Collection)

expense, it was never directly under the control of the Van Sweringen enterprises. Like the rest of the group, however, it was built on air rights over the property of the Cleveland Union Terminals Company.

The cornerstone for the Post Office was laid on February 16, 1933, and the next day the marker was gone. It had disappeared overnight. The explanation to the mystery turned out to be simple. The cornerstone-laying ceremony had been rushed ahead of its schedule so that it could bear the name of the outgoing Herbert Hoover administration in Washington, D.C. After the ceremony

had been completed, construction workers removed the stone so that it would not be damaged by the work still needed. Later it would be permanently set into place.

Two and one-half years after construction had begun, on September 3, 1934, the formal dedication of the new facility took place. The dedication ceremonies were the focal point of a public celebration. The community had little else to cheer about during those deep days of the Great Depression. The dedicatory plaque placed in the Prospect Avenue lobby bears the names of members of the administration of Franklin D. Roosevelt, which had succeeded Hoover's to power. Thus the cornerstone and the dedication plaque give credit for sponsorship of the construction project to two different presidencies.

The new main Cleveland Post Office boasted a total of 494,000 square feet of space on six levels. Loading docks were located on West Sixth Street, which was also the entry point for a roadway which led down to the concourse level of the Union Terminal. Part of the passageway branched off to reach the taxi stand area. Another connected with the interior roadway which was located south of the Steam Concourse. It extended to the freight elevators that served the track level. There the mail was transferred to and from the trains.

From the exterior, one would judge that the Post Office building had four floors above ground level. There are, in fact, five floors. The top floor was windowless and served as the mechanical floor for the facility.

The first through the fourth floors were devoted to processing the mails. The first floor, the one most familiar to Greater Clevelanders, housed the main postal services lobby.

Entered from either Huron Road or Prospect Avenue, the main lobby ran the width of the building. On both sides, its marble walls were pierced by service windows to accommodate the public. Above the windows was a series of marble reliefs, executed by artist Frank Jirouch, which depicted the historical progress of mail

The post office site is ready in 1929. The tracks leading to the CUT station are visible on the lower level next to the passageway that led to the cab stand. (Shaker Historical Museum)

The Post Office (lower right) is nearing completion in 1933. Note the arrow pointing toward Cleveland Airport on top of Hotel Cleveland. (Bruce Young Collection)

delivery in the United States. The center of the lobby was fitted with customer service tables for postal patrons to complete their mailing tasks. The lobby also housed a philatelic boutique, which sold postal items to stamp hobbyists. Two murals graced the main entranceway. Painted by Cleveland artist Jack J. Greitzer, they illustrated the tasks of those working in the building to prepare the mails for delivery.

The remainder of the first floor was set aside as the processing center for mail in the downtown delivery zones. The second, third, and fourth floors were used for

handling the mails for the rest of the Cleveland postal region. Administrative offices for the postal system were also situated on these floors. Honeycombed throughout the building were "secret passages" with viewing portals from which postal inspectors could supervise the operation and at the same time serve as an effective deterrent to theft.

The main Post Office was a busy building. It processed mail for a geographic area which stretched from Conneaut, Ohio, on the east to Vermillion, Ohio, on the west, and south to the borders of Summit County. Incoming mail was handled for five sectional areas comprising postal zipcodes 439 through 447 (Cleveland and its many suburban branches constitute zipcode area 441).

The Post Office Building was designed to provide a great deal of flexibility. That feature proved a real asset because the manner of working with the mails changed dramatically following the 1930s. What had begun as a chiefly hand-sorting process evolved into a technology-driven one. Huge and complex arrays of machinery greatly sped mail processing. Yet with the volume of mail constantly increasing (by 1980 an average one million pieces were handled each day by the main Post Office), and with trucks having replaced the railroads as the key components in the intercity delivery process, it became clear to postal authorities that major changes were required. Even the

addition in 1954 of the Parcel Post Annex on the lakefront did not significantly alter the realization that the main Post Office facility was no longer able to provide for future growth needs. The lack of adequate parking for Post Office trucks and the building's multi-floor design made the venue no longer practical in view of modern mail sorting practices.

In the late 1960s postal authorities decided that Cleveland needed a new main Post Office. They envisioned a grand opening for the new center in 1971. That hope, however, was overly optimistic. In fact, a series of problems and delays set the date back another eleven years.

Despite its plans for a new building, the United States Postal Service (its new name as of 1971) did not hesitate to do its duty when, on January 2, 1976, a six-ton slab of the sandstone facing fell

The marble-walled Post Office lobby stretched between Huron Road and Prospect Avenue. The style of the room is art deco. (United States Postal Service)

Lining the walls of the main lobby are a series of engravings by artist Frank Jirouch depicting the many steps in the process of delivering the U.S. mails. (Cleveland Landmarks Press Collection)

from the Post Office building, crushing an unoccupied automobile parked below.

A careful examination revealed that other slabs were also loosened, probably caused by years of vibration from the heavy vehicles passing over the bridges which surrounded the building. Safety dictated that repairs be made.

Since the Post Office formed one part of the Historic Register designation that the U. S. Department of the Interior had conferred on the entire Terminal Complex in 1976, law stipulated that the exterior design features of the building be preserved. The Postal Service committed itself to a total resurfacing of the building.

Beginning in 1976, most of the original sandstone facing was removed and replaced by sections of pre-cast concrete.

Those sections of the original facing which bore ornamental detail were removed, cleaned, and then hoisted back into position. The refacing project, at a total cost of just over $2 million, was completed in 1979.

The last day for the old Post Office Building came on April 3, 1982. The new facility, named in 1988 for Cleveland civil rights advocate John O. Holly, was located in the area framed by Orange and Broadway avenues, between East 14th and East 30th streets. Though only half the size of the old building and built with only one floor, it was designed to handle both parcel and regular mail. The efficiencies gained by the modern machinery used in handling the mail made the smaller space all that was necessary.

A postal worker tries to keep up with the steady stream of packages arriving on the conveyer belt. (Cleveland *Press* Collection of the Cleveland State University Libraries)

These two photos show the before (top) and after (bottom) look of the Post Office when it became necessary to replace the facing of the building. (United States Postal Service, top, and Cleveland Landmarks Press Collection, bottom)

When the Post Office moved into its new facility, the old building became surplus property. Federal law dictates that surplus governmental property be first offered to the General Services Administration (GSA) for its use. If the property is not claimed by that agency, it is, in turn, to be offered next to the state, then to the county, city, and the school system. If none of the governmental entities is interested, the property can then be placed out on bids to any interested party.

It turned out that no government agency was interested in the huge facility. The State of Ohio had just opened its new Lausche State Office Building, the city had built a new headquarters for its utilities department, and the school board, in a time of declining enrollment, had ample office and storage space available in school buildings that were being mothballed. While the County was feeling the pinch for space, it was not yet ready to commit to the considerable expense that would have been involved in renovating a building that had functioned more like an industrial plant than an office setting.

Forest City Enterprises, which had consolidated its ownership of the adjacent Union Terminal and Terminal Tower properties in 1982, saw the advantage of being able to manage the redevelopment of the old post office. In May 1983, Forest City, in partnership with the Roulston Company, announced its intention to buy the building and to develop it into a medical mart. The deal was completed on September 28, 1983, and for a modest $1.8

To convert the building to office use, it was necessary to carve two light courts into the interior. Work is in progress. (J. Janos photo, Forest City Enterprises)

127

million the Post Office Building was added to the Forest City real estate portfolio. Plans for use of the building as a medical merchandise mart, however, had to be abandoned when Cleveland Clinic, which had earlier expressed some interest in the project, withdrew from the plan.

Despite that setback, Forest City Enterprises decided to go ahead with its plans to renovate the structure, but the new thinking was that it should be converted into modern office space. That posed some significant challenges. The building's large floor plan meant that the interior space received virtually no sunlight, a feature that would limit potential interest in the building. The Cleveland architectural firm of van Dijk, Johnson & Partners was challenged to find a solution to the problem while at the same time respecting the Historic Register designation of the building.

The answer came by cutting two skylighted atriums into the center portion of the building. The glass-walled atriums allowed natural light to reach the interior of all five floors. One atrium was built immediately adjacent to the old Post Office lobby. This required carefully cutting out part of the old lobby wall. Since that space was historically protected, it was necessary to remove each of the huge wall sections in one piece. They were then turned 90 degrees to frame an entry to the new atrium space. This first floor of the lobby atrium became a public area; the second atrium, located closer to West Sixth Street, was reserved for tenant use.

Other changes were also made. Because of the building's high ceilings, it became possible to add a mezzanine level

between the first and second floors. A new entrance leading up to the Postal Lobby was also added. It is entered from West Third Street, directly across from the Ritz-Carlton Hotel. The Plaza can also be reached directly from Tower City Center or from the indoor parking facility beneath it, located in the area formerly occupied by the cab stand. The Greitzer murals and the Jirouch panels were all preserved in place.

Officials from Cleveland's MK-Ferguson Company were intrigued by the potential of the building. A major engineering and construction company, MK-Ferguson was in need of a large space to consolidate its 1,200-member workforce, and the large floor plans appealed to the company's need for spacious drafting areas. The company moved into the rehabilitated building in January 1991. While MK-Ferguson later was reorganized as Washington Group International, and the building attracted other tenants as well, it has retained it MK-Ferguson Plaza name.

The extensive work needed to convert the dark and dingy Post Office space into the modern business setting it became was expensive. It carried a $50 million price tag ($67 million in 2004 dollars).

The MK-Ferguson Plaza was yet another successful Tower City example of adaptive re-use for a historically significant structure. The rehabilitation of the old Post Office returned the gleam to yet another of the Terminal Complex gems. It represented one more triumph for the vision which Forest City Enterprises brought to the challenge of preserving and enhancing Cleveland's most significant downtown property.

CLEVELAND'S TOWERING TREASURE

In converting the Post Office into the MK-Ferguson Plaza, the architecture of the postal lobby was preserved, but a new entrance was created (center left) and the west wall (right) was opened to provide access to the new public atrium. (Forest City Enterprises)

The glass-walled atrium brought natural light into the center of the newly reconfigured office structure. (Richard Karberg photo)

The Department Store

chapter 8

As great a success as the Tower City Center plan has been, there yet remains one major problem to resolve. The home of Cleveland's newest and longest-surviving downtown department store, The Higbee Building, stands almost completely empty, the victim of changing shopping patterns and the inexorable out-migration of city residents to the ever more distant suburbs. Only in the future will the next phase in the life of this once vital cog in downtown commerce unfold.

On the day that the Terminal Tower was formally dedicated, June 28, 1930, there was still a yawning hole in the ground where The Higbee Company's new downtown store was to stand.

The department store building, when it was completed a little more than a year later, represented the newest major retail facility in the city. It was also the newest home of Cleveland's oldest major department store company.

It was September 1860 when the firm of Hower and Higbee opened for business on Superior Avenue, just west of Public Square. In 1902, following the death of

co-founder John Hower, surviving partner Edward Higbee had the store's name shortened to The Higbee Company.

The business was thriving, and it soon needed more space. In 1910, the 50th anniversary of the store's founding, Higbee's moved to a new and much larger building at Euclid Avenue and East 13th Street, right across the street from the rival Halle Bros. department store, where its business continued to prosper.

Having a department store as part of their Terminal Complex had been a key part of the Van Sweringen brothers' plans. But who were they to find to occupy the planned space? Their efforts to convince the owners of the major downtown stores fell on deaf ears, and so the Vans resorted to a tactic that they had successfully tried

The Higbee Company was located on Euclid Avenue at East 13th Street until the Van Sweringen brothers bought the company and relocated it to their Terminal Complex in 1931. (Cleveland Union Terminal Archives of the Cleveland State University Libraries)

131

in the past. In 1929 the Van Sweringen brothers purchased The Higbee Company for $7.5 million, and assigned its ownership to their Cleveland Terminals Building Company. With the department store company now in the fold, the brothers were able to proceed with planning its new home.

Once again the brothers chose as architect the firm of Graham, Anderson, Probst & White. The proposed department store was to be the largest built in the United States over the previous two decades. At a cost of $10 million, the huge new facility was intended to be the epitome of modern retail merchandising concepts in an atmosphere that more resembled the private club than the public market. Rich wooden paneling through-

out the store gave it an atmosphere of quality and class.

The Higbee store was huge. Rising 12 stories, it contained over one million square feet of floor space. It promoted its merchandise in 77 display windows, and whisked its customers from floor to floor on 20 elevators or by a set of wooden escalators. The location of the elevator lobbies and escalator corridor was a prime example of the careful planning that went into the store's layout. They were located in the center of the store, yet arranged in such a way as not to intrude on the most effective use of floor space. Because the main floor and the Prospect level shared what constituted one full floor in the stories above, it was possible to situate the elevator-escalator corridor to one side, leaving the entire main sales area unobstructed. Equivalent space on the upper floors was evenly divided by the central location of the elevator-escalator lobby.

Built adjoining the Terminal Tower, and bounded by Ontario Street on the east, Prospect Avenue on the south, and Public Square on the north, the Higbee store's exterior design and materials blended well with the other buildings in the complex. Though different in several details, the department store effectively served as a balance to the Hotel Cleveland building which flanked the Tower to the west.

Besides easy access from three streets, the store also benefitted from its connection with the other Terminal buildings. One entrance opened from the Portico of the Tower; another was via the Prospect Arcade, and a third connected directly to the Union Terminal's concourse level. The basement entrance stood at the end of the passageway which connected the concourse to the Prospect Buildings to the south, making shopping at Higbee's convenient for workers in those buildings

as well. The basement store entrance was just steps away from the Shaker Rapid traction concourse turnstiles, and so it had additional appeal for shoppers from the Heights area.

The large size of the new building allowed The Higbee Company, for the first time in its history, to be a complete department store. It provided space for several new departments that were not a part of its

Structural steel for the new Higbee department store has reached the 10th floor in January 1931. (Cleveland Union Terminal Archives of the Cleveland State University Libraries)

The Higbee Company's new store is almost complete. A passage from the store's top floor connected with the Terminal Tower, making access to the department store and its 10th floor Silver Grille convenient for workers in the neighboring building. (Cleveland Union Terminal Archives of the Cleveland State University Libraries)

The Higbee store's interior had the ambiance of a fine club. The elevator lobbies were paneled in dark wood. (Cleveland Landmarks Press Collection)

Higbee's was always beautifully decorated for the Christmas shopping season. (Jay Himes Collection)

East 13th Street offerings. New departments included housewares, furniture, glassware, carpeting, and sporting goods. The addition of a basement store also meant that Higbee's could compete more effectively with The May Company and The Bailey Company, located just across Ontario Street. Both of those stores had monopolized the trade of the thrifty shopper. A tenth-floor Auditorium permitted

the store to provide a series of programs of interest to customers, and the adjacent Silver Grille restaurant allowed them to dine comfortably (for a complete history of The Silver Grille, cf. Karberg in reference list)..

The public eagerly awaited the new store's opening. Full page advertisements in the city's newspapers had kept shoppers abreast of the building's progress. The advertisements proclaimed that the store would be filled with $5 million of new merchandise. Almost nothing, neither equipment nor merchandise, was brought over from the old Euclid Avenue store.

Finally the building was ready. The lines were already long by the time the store opened its doors on Tuesday morning, September 8, 1931. Throughout the day customers continued to pour into the store, exceeding even the most optimistic of expectations. By the time the store closed that evening, checkers at the doors had tallied a staggering total of 359,079 first-day patrons.

That first-day crowd, however, was a one-time phenomenon. The Great Depression curbed shopping, and the dearth of customers soon impacted the store's solvency. The Higbee store, just as the rest of the Van Sweringen empire, soon foundered. In 1937, John P. Murphy and Charles L. Bradley, long-time associates of the Vans, acquired all the Higbee common stock. Bradley became Higbee's president, remaining in that post until his death in 1944. He was succeeded by Murphy, who led the store until 1968. Under their leadership the store recovered to become a thriving and profitable enterprise (for a complete history

of the Higbee Company, cf. Karberg in reference list).

The hallmarks of the entire Terminal group's design were wise planning of space and solid construction. Little in the way of major reconstruction was required to keep the store in tune with the changing needs of the shopping public. During the entire Higbee era, only one major renovation was undertaken. In 1956, sensitive to the needs of its shoppers and concerned about the growing trend towards suburban shopping, Higbee's decided to modernize the store. A second set of moving stairways replaced the northern elevator lobby, and the second through the fifth floors were remodeled to give them a more contemporary look.

Since the city's founding, shopping meant going downtown. But by 1960, as population began to shift from the city to the suburbs and as the private automobile replaced reliance on public transportation, large outlying shopping strips (and later enclosed malls) took a toll on the downtown retail shopping trade. Three of the six downtown department stores closed, William Taylor and Sons in 1961, The Bailey Company in 1962, and Sterling Lindner in 1968. The Halle Bros. store survived until 1982. That left only two downtown department stores, The May Company and The Higbee Company (for a complete history of downtown department stores and shops, cf. Karberg and Toman in reference list).

Higbee officials understood that no matter how much they might value the downtown flagship store, that bottom-line considerations required expansion into the suburban market. In 1961 the firm opened its first branch store in the Westgate Shopping Center, and over the next 20 years, the chain grew to 14 stores in all.

For many years during the Christmas season, Higbee's main floor decoration featured large bells in the central archway. (Cleveland *Press* Collection of the Cleveland State University Libraries)

Holiday shoppers examine the store's first floor cosmetic and fragrances department. (Jack Muslovski photo, Cleveland Landmarks Press Collection)

Higbee's ran a first-rate book department on its fifth floor. This is how the department looked following the 1956 renovations. (Cleveland *Press* Collection of the Cleveland State University Libraries)

From the time the Tower City Center plans first surfaced, Herbert Strawbridge, president of The Higbee Company since 1968, was a strong supporter. He viewed the proposed retail mall and his department store as being of mutual benefit. Local control of Higbee's, however, came to an end in 1987 when the Higbee chain was sold to Brierly Investments of New Zealand, which in turn sold the chain to a joint venture of Dillard's Department Stores of Little Rock, Arkansas, and the DeBartolo Development Company of Youngstown, Ohio. After studying the Higbee operation, Dillard's tended to view the shops and restaurants of the Tower City development as competition rather than complement. They feared that The Avenue would siphon customers from the department store. As a result, Dillard's decided to downsize the store to five floors, eliminate all food service, and reconfigure the bargain basement department into a

new men's store. The top floor for store operations would be the fourth.

The fifth through the twelfth floors were to be converted to office space. Early in 1990 demolition proceeded on the upper floors of the building, but though the space was readied for future use, those floors

The 10th floor Higbee Auditorium was the scene for many programs, from fashion shows to book lectures. (Cleveland Landmarks Press Collection)

The Silver Grille was one of the city's most popular dining rooms. It closed in 1989 when Dillard's took over the store. After Forest City Enterprises purchased the Higbee Building, the Silver Grille space was lovingly restored. It was rededicated in May 2002, and is now used for private parties. (Richard E. Karberg photo)

The 10th floor elevator lobby was also saved as part of the historic preservation tax credit program. This is the scene that today greets visitors to the Silver Grille. (Richard E. Karberg photo)

have remained largely empty, with the exception of some space on the seventh floor occupied by a few telecommunication companies.

Happily the gutting of the upper floors had one exception, the abandoned Silver Grille space. The building's historic desig-

nation and the tax credits used by the Dillard/DeBartolo partnership protected three parts of the structure: the exterior, the first floor, and the Silver Grille space.

On January 31, 1992, The May Company closed its downtown store. That left Higbee's, renamed that year as Dillard's, the last surviving downtown department store.

Despite reducing the store's selling area, Dillard's found operating the giant building expensive. In 1992 Forest City Enterprises purchased a half-share in the building, hoping thereby to solidify the Dillard occupancy, and in 2001 it bought out the remaining share of ownership held by Dillard's. Forest City officials did everything they could to retain Dillard's as a tenant for the downtown building, but those efforts were ultimately in vain. Downtown department stores were an endangered species. In fact, the Cleveland store was the last downtown store still operated by the 339-store Dillard chain. Its days were numbered.

Dillard's gutted most of the space from the fifth floor up to prepare it for possible conversion to office use. The huge floors have stood empty since 1990. (Richard E. Karberg photo)

The Higbee store was chosen as the site for the 1983 movie, *A Christmas Story.* This is the outdoor scene created for the film. (Richard E. Karberg Collection)

The dreaded announcement came on November 12, 2001: The store would close on December 31. The downtown store had served Greater Clevelanders for just over 70 years, and more than a few of its customers shed a tear at its passing. For most Clevelanders, the Higbee Company's downtown store represented a treasure trove of happy memories, such as the annual Christmas season visit to meet Santa Claus or patronize the Twigbee Shop. They fondly recall the store's wonderful window displays and the interior holiday decorations which made it a fairyland of glittering lights. They remember fashion shows and book-and-author programs in the Auditorium. They recall the intriguing annual Import Fairs. They reminisce over being treated as children to a dress-up lunch at the Silver Grille where their meal was presented in a toy stove. They still recall the basement store's soda fountain which served a "frosted malted,"

so delightfully thick that it seemed it would last forever.

With the departure of Dillard's, Forest City Enterprises was left with a daunting task, what to do with one million square feet of space. An answer to that problem has not yet surfaced, but Forest City Enterprises, recognizing the historic significance of the space, returned the building to its longtime name, reaffixing the old Higbee Company plaques to the building's main entranceways. It also completed a wonderful restoration of the historic Silver Grille space on the 10th floor, and created two new entrances to reach it, one from the third level of the Avenue's Tower Court, and the other from Prospect Avenue. The Silver Grille space is now operated as a catering center, with the Ritz-Carlton hotel providing the food service.

The rest of the store awaits a future still undetermined.

Epilog

On March 17, 1976, the Cleveland Union Terminal Group was placed on the National Register of Historic Places. While the distinction was welcomed, for Greater Clevelanders it was hardly necessary. For them, the importance of the Terminal Group needed no official imprimatur. Ever since the steel skeleton of the Terminal Tower had first pierced the downtown skyline, the citizens of Cleveland knew that they were gaining a monument befitting its Sixth City status and its manufacturing and industrial might. Clevelanders were proud of their city, and in 1930 the Terminal Group gave that pride a tangible expression. Almost instantly the Terminal Tower became the city's most important symbol. Seventy-five years later, that has not changed.

This really is what The Cleveland *Press* editorial meant when it said that "A city writes its epics not in words, but in stone and steel." The Terminal Group has been Cleveland's epic story.

It personified Daniel Burnham's maxim: "Make big plans; aim high in hope and work, remembering that a noble, logical plan once recorded will never die, but long after we are gone will be a living thing asserting itself with growing insistence."

It has been 70 years since the authors of the grand Terminal epic, Oris P. and Mantis J. Van Sweringen died, but their legacy lives on. The Vans had vision. Cleveland will never forget them.

Though the Vans were long gone, their vision retained the capacity to inspire. Onto the scene came the Ratner and Miller families of Forest City Enterprises. They fully comprehended the significance of the Union Terminal complex, and though they recognized how challenging it would be to reconfigure the property to address contemporary needs, they did not blanch at the prospect. Their vision was matched by their commitment to the city they proudly called home. Tower City Center is their legacy.

As the Terminal Tower Complex celebrates its diamond anniversary, it remains the city's symbol and its most famous landmark. Its stone and steel remind all Greater Clevelanders of their city's proud past. Its 75-year history illuminates a path to a future bright with promise.

The Terminal Tower is the scene of many civic celebrations. Here fireworks create the background for a Tower silhouette. (David Kachinko photo)

References

Christiansen, H. (1965). *Northern Ohio's Interurbans and Rapid Transit Railways*. Cleveland: Transit Data.

The Cleveland Union Terminals Company & The Cleveland Terminals Building Company. (1930—reprinted 1979). *The Union Station*. Cleveland: Robert J. Liederbach, publisher.

Condon, G. E. (1967). *Cleveland: The Best Kept Secret*. New York: Doubleday.

Cook, R. J. (1991). *New York Central's Mercury*. Lynchburg, VA: TLC Publishing.

Deegan, G. G. & Toman, J. A. (1999). *The Heart of Cleveland: Public Square in the 20th Century*. Cleveland: Cleveland Landmarks Press.

Grabowski, J. J. & Leedy, W. C. (1990). *Tower City Center: A Historical Perspective*. Cleveland: Western Reserve Historical Society.

Haberman, I. S. (1979). *The Van Sweringens of Cleveland: Biography of an Empire*. Cleveland: Western Reserve Historical Society.

Harwood, H. H., Jr. (2003). *Invisible Giants: The Empires of Cleveland's Van Sweringen Brothers*. Bloomington, IN: Indiana University Press.

Herrick, C., Jr. (1986). *Cleveland Landmarks*. Cleveland: Landmarks Publishing Company.

Johanesson, E. (1979). *Cleveland Architecture, 1876-1976*. Cleveland: Western Reserve Historical Society.

Johanesson, E. (1999). *A Cleveland Legacy: The Architecture of Walker and Weeks*. Kent, OH: Kent State University Press.

Karberg, R. E. (2001). *The Higbee Company and the Silver Grille*. Cleveland: Cleveland Landmarks Press.

Karberg, R. E. (2002). *The Silver Grille* (rev. ed.). Cleveland: Cleveland Landmarks Press.

Karberg R. E. & Toman, J. A. (2002). *Euclid Avenue: Cleveland's Sophisticated Lady, 1920-1970*. Cleveland: Cleveland Landmarks Press.

Kiefer, G. W. (2000). *Steel & Real Estate: Margaret Bourke-White and Corporate Culture in Cleveland 1927-1929*. Wooster, OH: College of Wooster Art Museum.

Leedy, W. C. (1983). "Cleveland's Terminal Tower: The Van Sweringens' Afterthought." In *The Gamut Looks at Cleveland*. Cleveland: Cleveland State University.

Rose, W. G. (1950). *Cleveland: The Making of a City*. Cleveland: World Publishing.

Schofield, M. P., 1976. *Landmark Architecture of Cleveland*, Pittsburgh, Ober Park Associates.

Toman, J. A. (1989). *The Shaker Heights Rapid Transit*. Glendale, CA: Interurban Press.

Toman, J. A. & Cook, D. J. (1980). *The Terminal Tower Complex, 1930-1980*. Cleveland: Cleveland Landmarks Press.

Toman, J. A. & Hays, B. S. (1996). *Horse Trails to Regional Rails: The Story of Public Transit in Cleveland*. Kent, OH: Kent State University Press.

Index